The Man,
The Music,
The Message
BOB DYLAN

The Man,
The Music,
The Message

BOB
By
Don
Williams
DYLAN

Fleming H. Revell Company
Old Tappan, New Jersey

Unless otherwise identified, Scripture quotations in this book are from the King James Version of the Bible.

Scripture quotations identified NAS are from the New American Standard Bible, © The Lockman Foundation 1960, 1962, 1963, 1968, 1971, 1972, 1973, 1975, 1977.

Scripture quotation identified RSV is from the Revised Standard Version of the Bible, copyrighted 1946, 1952, © 1971 and 1973.

Excerpts reprinted by permission of Grosset & Dunlap from BOB DYLAN: AN INTIMATE BIOGRAPHY, copyright © 1971 by Anthony Scaduto.

Excerpts from ROLLING THUNDER LOGBOOK by Sam Shepard are Copyright © 1977 by Sam Shepard. Reprinted by permission of Viking Penguin Inc.

Lyrics from "Diamonds and Rust" by Joan Baez are copyright © Chandos Music (ASCAP). Used by permission.

Excerpts from "Dylan Makes Another Stunning Comeback," by Christopher Connelly, from *Rolling Stone*, Nov. 24, 1983, by Straight Arrow Publishers, Inc., © 1983. All Rights Reserved. Reprinted by Permission.

Excerpts from "The Rolling Stone Interview: Bob Dylan," by Kurt Loder, from *Rolling Stone*, June 21, 1984, by Straight Arrow Publishers, Inc., © 1984. All Rights Reserved. Reprinted by Permission.

Excerpts from "Bob Dylan and Our Times: The Slow Train Is Coming," by Jann Wenner, from *Rolling Stone*, Sept. 20, 1979, by Straight Arrow Publishers, Inc., © 1979. All Rights Reserved. Reprinted by Permission.

Excerpts from "Dylan's New Furor: Rock 'n' Religion," by Robert Hillburn, are Copyright 1979, *Los Angeles Times*. Reprinted by permission.

Excerpts from "Dylan's Evangelicalism Goes On," by Robert Hillburn, are Copyright 1979, *Los Angeles Times*. Reprinted by permission.

Excerpts from "Dylan: 'I Learned That Jesus Is Real and I Wanted That,' " by Robert Hillburn, are Copyright 1980, *Los Angeles Times*. Reprinted by permission.

Excerpts from "Bob Dylan at 42—Rolling Down Highway 61 Again," by Robert Hillburn, are Copyright 1983, *Los Angeles Times*. Reprinted by permission.

Excerpts from "Dylan: The View From '84," by Robert Hillburn, are Copyright 1984, *Los Angeles Times*. Reprinted by permission.

The photo on pages 11, 25, 49, 75, 109, 133, and 151 is Copyright ©1984 Los Angeles Times/ Patrick Downs.

Acknowledgments continued on page 159.

Library of Congress Cataloging in Publication Data

Williams, Don.
    Bob Dylan: the man, the music, the message.

    Bibliography: p.
    1. Dylan, Bob, 1941–   —Religion. 2. Singers—
United States—Biography. I. Title.
    ML420.D98W54   1985   784.4'924 [B]   85-8307
    ISBN 0-8007-1439-3

For Kathryn
my "Covenant Woman"

Contents

Preface

This is a very personal book. I was introduced to the music of Bob Dylan in 1966 by my friend Bob Marlowe in Hollywood, California. Bob forced me to listen to Dylan's records and then plunked out the tunes on his thirty-dollar guitar. It was a moment of truth for me. Suddenly, I began to hear a generation. I was a young college pastor working with USC and UCLA fraternity and sorority types—and my eyes were opened to a new world.

Shortly thereafter, on a Sunday night at the Hollywood Presbyterian Church, we held a service entitled "The Gospel According to Bob Dylan." The *Los Angeles Free Press* photographed the marquee announcement, publishing it on its back-page calendar. Over a thousand hippies, freaks, addicts, hustlers, groupies, and students showed up to hear Dylan's protest music. It was clear—we were on to something, and there was no turning back.

Dylan would take me to the streets of Hollywood. It would mean a coffeehouse—The Salt Company—crash pads, marches down the Boulevard. It would mean fighting for the lives of drug addicts, seeing pregnant mothers through the births of unwanted children, counseling gays battling with their brokenness, going before draft boards to support claims for conscientious objector status, standing with students striking on their campuses.

All of that has faded into the past. Dylan has not. His songs over the years have captivated my attention. His lyrics have haunted me. His concerts have enthralled me. His conversion staggered me. I admit my bias at the outset. Bob Dylan is one of the unique, formative people in my life. I owe him a deep, personal debt of gratitude. Thus, this book comes from almost two decades of seeing the world, in many respects, through Dylan's eyes. Here I attempt to chart the course that he has taken. I hope to show that his conversion was no cop-out, but the only possible conclusion for a brilliant artist and thinker who had, one by one, exhausted his other options.

My thanks to many who have helped and encouraged me along the way in this study, especially Lance Bowen, Bob Papazian, Paul Westphal, Tim McCalmont, Mark Dawson, Peter Kenvin, Mark McCoy, and Tony Creed. They have kept me sharp and in the battle.

Chapter 1—Controversy

*"They ask me how I feel
And if my love is real
And how I know I'll make it through?"*

Bob Dylan's conversion fell like a bomb. It aroused the public, dismayed the critics, and angered the fans. More than six years later the controversy still rages.

The news of "born-again Bob" burst upon the pop music world in the fall of '79 as Dylan released his first Christian album, *Slow Train Coming*, and launched a West Coast tour. "Bob Dylan's God-Awful Gospel" headlined the *San Francisco Chronicle*. "Bob Dylan: His Show's a Real Drag," concurred the *San Francisco Examiner*. Despite the bad press, the *Los Angeles Times* reported, "Dylan's Evangelicalism Goes On" and then summed it all up: "Dylan's New Furor: Rock 'n' Religion."

Rolling Stone, oracle and chronicler of the rock world (which, incidentally, took its name from Dylan's song "Like a Rolling Stone"), summed up 1979 by recalling in its lead paragraph that "this was the year in which Jewish-born Bob Dylan finally found a reason to believe in Jesus."[1] The astonishment of many was further expressed by Robert Hilburn, critic for the *Los Angeles Times*, when he asked, "Who would ever have thought in the age of the Sex Pistols and punk rock that the most controversial issue in rock would be religion, and that Bob Dylan would be at the center of it?"[2]

Indeed, Dylan was not only *at* the center, he *was* the center. The controversy raged over Dylan himself. As *Newsweek* observed, not since Dylan went from acoustical to electric at the 1965 Newport Folk Festival had people been so confounded.

---

[1] "Random Notes 1979," *Rolling Stone*, 27 Dec. 1979–10 Jan. 1980, p. 93.
[2] Robert Hilburn, "Dylan's New Furor: Rock 'n' Religion," *Los Angeles Times*, 18 Nov. 1979, Calendar, p. 82.

"This time the storm centers not only on Dylan's music, but on his message: the 38-year-old former Robert Zimmerman, suddenly resurrected as a born-again Christian, is spouting religious fundamentalism to a rock 'n' roll beat."[3]

Could it be that Dylan was merely expanding on his long-recognized spiritual and mystical interests? Perhaps he was adopting a new genre for his music. Or was his "born-again" identification just a cheap commercial trick? Had Dylan assumed yet another one of his masks which he would later discard? Or had he suffered a "failure of nerve," a personal crisis that sent him fleeing into the shelter of an authoritarian fundamentalism?

Rumors of Dylan's change appeared first in the spring of '79 in the *Washington Post Magazine*. Gossip columnist Rudy Maxa reported that Dylan had "accepted Christ" and joined the Vineyard Christian Fellowship based in Southern California. This seemed to be supported by a deposition that Dylan gave in Beverly Hills in May as part of his defense in a defamation-of-character suit. *Rolling Stone* reported, "Questioned about his wealth and property, Dylan responded, 'You mean my treasure on earth?' And when asked if he was known by any other name, he replied, 'Not here. Not on this earth.' "[4]

The rumors seemed verified later in the summer with the release of his new album, *Slow Train Coming*. Here was Bob Dylan singing songs of faith. The jacket cover had a line drawing of a train moving down a track still under construction. The railroad worker's pick in the foreground formed a cross. On the back of the jacket there was a photograph of a ship's mast at sunset (or sunrise?). The mast symbolized a cross and a silhouetted figure seemed turned toward it. Dylan himself suggests that the cross, central to Christianity, is the key to *Slow Train Coming*. As he expressed it in one of the album cuts, "When You Gonna Wake Up":

> There's a man upon a cross
> And He's been crucified for you
> Believe in His power
> That's about all you got to do.

---

[3] "The (New) World According to Dylan," *Newsweek*, 17 Dec. 1979, p. 90.
[4] "Random Notes," *Rolling Stone*, 26 July 1979, p. 38.

Two weeks after its release, *Slow Train Coming* was hovering at number three on the pop charts. Half a million copies had been sold and Columbia reported continuing sales at 100,000 a week. Jann Wenner offered a major review in *Rolling Stone* and called the album probably Dylan's finest record musically. He writes, "Dylan's new songs are statements of strength and simplicity, and [they] . . . again equal his early classics."[5]

Wenner sees Dylan's songs in the historical perspective of his apocalyptic visions, biblical symbolism, "religious allegory," patriotism, love songs, and moral outrage. While he admits that the religious content of *Slow Train Coming* is pervasive, Wenner has not been convinced of Dylan's conversion. Similar to the grief process after a loved one's death, Wenner's first reaction is denial. He concludes, "But neither the album itself, nor any first-hand reports from the usual suspects, say that Dylan has been 'born again.' " In a later edition of *Rolling Stone*, Wenner warns against "fanatics and far-outs" who talk about this "so-called born-again album in order to create their latest image of Dylan."[6]

Alas, if *Slow Train Coming* left the critics questioning in '79, Dylan's tour would not. Here he threw down the gauntlet.

Starting in early November, Bob Dylan brought a cross between a rock 'n' roll concert and a black gospel service to concert halls. He chose to open in San Francisco, the city where a turned-on and dropped-out generation had been fed on the Dylan of the sixties. Did he owe the city a debt? There was one thing for certain. If his gospel concert would go here it would go anywhere.

Dylan began at the Warfield Theater on Market Street in the midst of porno shops and sleezy bars. The ornate stage glowed with amps as the old vaudeville hall filled to its 2,200 capacity. Most of the audience looked typical for San Francisco, dressed in army surplus. Joints were passed until the restlessness was broken by Regina Havis, from Dylan's black backup trio, who stepped to center stage. Softly, dramatically, she narrated a story about a poor old woman who was told by the Lord to go visit her dying son. When she was unable to ride the train because she

---

[5] Jann Wenner, "Bob Dylan and Our Times: The Slow Train Is Coming," *Rolling Stone*, 20 Sept. 1979, p. 95.
[6] Jann Wenner, "Best Albums of '79," *Rolling Stone*, 27 Dec. 1979–10 Jan. 1980, p. 124.

could afford no ticket, the conductor finally allowed her on board because, he said, "Old Woman, Jesus has got your ticket." Bang! The stage lights went up, the rest of the trio materialized, dressed in sequined flash, and three incredible voices belted out several gospel songs. The women created their own atmosphere, displaying remarkable vocal versatility and the power of their gospel lyrics, punctuating their set by an occasional, "Thank You, Jesus" and "Praise the Lord." The Warfield Theater in gay-grim San Francisco became First-Baptist-Church-For-A-Night.

Next, without pause, Bob Dylan, dressed down in a white shirt, black pants, and a leather jacket, stepped onto the stage with his band of lead guitar, bass, drums, piano, and organ. Starting with "Gotta Serve Somebody," Dylan seemed to bite out the words. He confronted his suspicious audience with their two alternatives: "It may be the Devil or it may be the Lord/But you gotta serve somebody," and went on to cover most of the songs on *Slow Train Coming.*

After another single from one of the trio, Dylan offered a new set of unrecorded songs, including lyrics like "I'm hanging on to the Solid Rock/Laid before the foundation of the world" and "I've been saved/By the blood of the Lamb." His singing was raspy, melodic, enchanting, severe. At times his face looked hard; at other times it seemed to glow. The last song in the second set was "In the Garden," an evangelical recitation of the gospel story. The final verse announces Jesus' rising from the dead and asks, "Do you believe?" Was this a rock concert?

The opening night press reported that the audience sat in stunned silence throughout most of the show, offering polite applause after each number. Some, however, booed or walked out, but most were shocked. Where were the old songs? The old war cries? The old lost loves? Bill Graham, the concert promoter and rock impresario, explained, "The public wasn't aware. We were all used to nostalgia, but this was something completely new."[7]

By the next night, however, Dylan received his first standing ovation. He responded with an encore-benediction, "Blessed Is the Name of the Lord Forever." After rocking out in praise, he closed alone at the piano singing, "I'm Pressin' On to the Higher Calling of My Lord."

---

[7] "Dylan Tour Off to Shaky Start," *Rolling Stone*, 13 Dec. 1979, p. 15.

The reports of the critics about Dylan's bombing turned out to be wishful thinking. As Bill Graham put it, "From night to night the show keeps getting stronger. It is awesome. I am a Jew, and I am deeply moved by what this man is doing. It's a very profound public display of personal convictions."[8] The San Francisco concerts were extended from seven to fourteen nights. Then Dylan moved on to Los Angeles and San Diego.

As the series progressed Dylan became more verbal. On opening night his only comment was, "I hope you were uplifted." Four nights later when someone called out for his old song, "Lay, Lady, Lay," Dylan smiled slightly and said (paraphrasing the Bible), "The old has passed away" (*see* 2 Corinthians 5:17). He also introduced his new song, "I'm Hanging on to the Solid Rock Laid Before the Foundation of the World," as a song for the end of the end times.[9]

Again, in San Francisco and elsewhere Dylan often commented, "We are here tonight by the power of God. That's the *only* power. That's what I believe."[10]

By the time he reached Los Angeles, Dylan was even more pointed than in San Francisco. Referring to the "Slow Train" he warned, "Christ will return to set up His Kingdom in Jerusalem. There really is a slow train coming, you know . . . and it is picking up speed."[11] Later Dylan said, "Some people call Satan the real God of this world. All you have to do is look around to see that's true. But I wonder how many of you know that Satan has been defeated by the cross?" Robert Hilburn of the *Los Angeles Times* notes, "When hundreds in the capacity (3,300) audience . . . cheered, Dylan smiled, looked at the gospel vocal trio and said, ''Well, it doesn't look like we're alone tonight.' " Dylan also concluded, "This isn't a concert in the regular sense . . . 'cause we're here to give all praise and glory unto God."[12] Dylan didn't bother to explain that his series also wasn't a concert in the regular sense because all of the proceeds went to World Vision's overseas relief work, rather than the performer's pocket.

Later, in San Diego, Dylan advised, "If you don't know

[8] Ibid.
[9] This concert was attended by the author. This song is now titled "Solid Rock" on *Saved.*
[10] Hilburn, "Dylan's New Furor: Rock 'n' Religion," p. 82.
[11] Robert Hilburn, "Dylan's Evangelicalism Goes On," *Los Angeles Times,* 20 Nov. 1979, pt. V, p. 1.
[12] Ken Tucker, "Dylan's Slow Train of Thought," *Los Angeles Herald Examiner,* 20 Nov. 1979, Style, p. 1.

Dylan begins his controversial "Slow Train" concert series at the Warfield Theater in San Francisco in November 1979. With him is Tim Drummond of his backup band.

Jesus, you might check into it. Is He real? Or IS HE REAL." At the end of the final San Diego concert, Dylan reported, "People say, 'Bob, don't do that stuff.' It may be costing me a lot of fans. Maybe I'll have to start singing on street corners. Still, I'll give all the praise and glory to God."

Doubts about the genuineness of Dylan's conversion were banished by this tour. In his first public appearance after *Slow Train Coming*, Bob Dylan transformed concert halls into sanctuaries with his own special blend of rock concert and revival meeting. His gospel trio set the stage, and with a radical break from the past, he sang only his gospel music. The re-created Dylan re-created his concerts accordingly. Later he would integrate the old songs with the new, but for now, in this apocalyptic moment, the statement would be clear and unequivocal.

As it said farewell to 1979, *Rolling Stone* editorialized that, "Dylanologists are shocked and saddened by . . . [Dylan's] apparent conversion to Christianity."[13] But why all this outcry? Why this incessant attention to one man's spiritual odyssey?

At the heart of this compulsion about Bob Dylan is the fact that he, more than anyone else, created a generation. This makes him a man of mythic proportions, beyond mere fame as a rock 'n' roll superstar. Virtually single-handedly Dylan gave the watershed decade of the sixties its education.

It was Dylan who made marching, rioting students' moral outrage definitive. It was Dylan who ripped through the establishment's grim hypocrisy, elevating raw rebellion by brilliant critique. It was Dylan who comforted the brokenhearted by his own inner chaos and grief. It was Dylan who experimented with new worlds and became the troubadour of what he found. The voices of King and Kennedy were silenced, but not Dylan's. This alone makes his every move and phase significant to the generation that found its soul in union with his. As those who have inherited a culture so decisively impacted by Dylan, how then are we to understand his power and continuing legacy?

To begin with, Dylan is a musical genius. It was Dylan who made folk music commercial and then created the rebirth of rock by uniting folk's message music to rock's elemental energy. At

---

[13] *Rolling Stone*, 27 Dec. 1979–10 Jan. 1980, p. 79.

last, substantial issues could be addressed to a mass audience and burned into the brains of millions of listeners. Editorial control of the music media was taken from the hands of the adult professionals once and for all, and Dylan led the way.

Then, too, in the words of Michael Gray, "Dylan is the greatest rock 'n' roll star in the world." Gray continues, "Partly, of course, this is because he's the best rock writer and singer and performer there has ever been; but partly—and the two aren't by any means totally distinguishable—it's because he's become an idol, a superstar."[14]

From a sheer statistical review, this judgment can be amply supported. In fact, Dylan has commanded the attention and adulation of millions from the early sixties to the present. A majority of his commercial albums have been certified as "gold" with sales of over $1 million each. On top is *Highway 61 Revisited* with over 20 million copies pressed. Moreover, Dylan continues to be a touring musician. When he put on a series of nationwide concerts in 1974, there were 20 million requests for the 651,000 available seats. Four years later a quarter of a million people came to Blackbushe (England) for one concert. It is here, as a performer, that Dylan's consummate power is seen.

Sam Shepard, who accompanied Dylan on his Northeastern concert odyssey, "The Rolling Thunder Review" in 1975–76, described the musician's magic in the *Rolling Thunder Logbook*. At the Seacrest Hotel in Falmouth, Massachusetts, in an impromptu concert late one night, Dylan broke through to hundreds of middle-aged Jewish women engrossed in a Chinese form of dominoes called Mah-Jongg. After his companion, poet Allen Ginsberg, unsettled the crowd by a long, uncomfortable reading, Dylan took the stage. Shepard reports, "Leave aside his lyrical genius for a second and just watch this transformation of energy which he carries. Only a few minutes ago the place was deadly thick with tension and embarrassment, and now he's blown the top right off it. He's infused the room with a high feeling of life-giving excitement. It's not the kind of energy that drives people off the deep end but the kind that brings courage and hope and

---

[14] Michael Gray, *The Art of Bob Dylan* (New York: St. Martin's Press, 1981), pp. 108–109.

above all things brings life pounding into the foreground. If he can do it here, in the dead of winter, at an off-season seaside resort . . ., then it's no wonder he can rock the nation."[15]

Shepard goes on to reflect on Dylan's greatness. He says that Dylan plays for "Big Stakes." His art falls upon us as questions, speaking to the emotions, moving us into an area of mystery. "Dylan creates a mystic atmosphere out of the land around us. The land we walk on every day and never see until someone shows it to us." Dylan commands his music like a magician and as he weaves his magic "now it's not the eyes that see him. It's the heart." Shepard questions reflectively, "What is this strange, haunted environment he creates on stage, on record, on film, on everything he touches? What world is he drawing from and drawing us all into as a result? It's right here in front of us, but no one can touch it."

Paul Nelson sums up Dylan's contribution: "It is hard to claim too much for the man who in every sense revolutionized modern poetry, American folk music, popular music, and the whole of modern-day thought; even the strongest praise seems finally inadequate. Not many contemporary artists have the power to actually change our lives, but surely Dylan does—and has."[16]

This, then, helps us to understand the angry storm that broke over Dylan's turn to Christianity. It also helps us to understand why the controversy has not abated.

After two more albums—*Saved* in 1980 and *Shot of Love* in 1981—in what the press dubbed his Slow Train Era, Dylan fell silent. Later concert tours saw him mix his Christian music with his older work. *CREEM* magazine reported in March of '82 that Dylan filled Music Hall in Cincinnati "to the brim." He opened his show with "Gotta Serve Somebody," "the initial public musical message of his conversion to Christianity back in '79," and then went on to balance his "born again religious numbers" with older songs. That same month, *New York Magazine* speculated that Dylan's attending his son's bar mitzvah rather than presenting the "Gospel Song of the Year" award for the National

---

[15] Sam Shepard, *Rolling Thunder Logbook* (New York: Penguin Books, 1977), pp. 31–32.
[16] Paul Nelson, "Bob Dylan Approximately," in *Bob Dylan: A Restrospective,* ed. Craig McGregor (New York: William Morrow, 1972), p. 172.

Music Publishers' Association meant that he was going back to Judaism.

A year later, as he put the finishing touches on *Infidels*, Dylan granted a late-night interview to Martin Keller in New York City. In it, Dylan avoided any direct statement about his spiritual convictions: "People want to know where I'm at because they don't know where they're at." As he often does, Dylan warned about religion, "You can turn anything into a religious context. Religion is a dirty word. It doesn't mean anything. Coca-Cola is a religion. Oil and steel are a religion. In the name of religion, people have been raped, killed and defiled. Today's religion is tomorrow's bondage." When asked, however, if he was returning to his "Jewish roots," Dylan responded with a brief biblical narration of his true Jewish roots—he is like those attacked as outlaws by the ruling powers in ancient Israel (see, for example, King Saul's attempts to kill David). He is like those Hebrew prophets who told the truth and whose brethren wanted "to bust their brains for telling it right like it is." These are his roots. Dylan went on, "I ain't looking for them in synagogues with six-pointed Egyptian stars shining down from every window, I can tell you that much."[17]

With the release of his new album *Infidels*, then, in the fall of '83, a sigh of relief was heard across the media and quickly echoed by untold numbers of fans. Recent rumors seemed right: Dylan had given up his "born-again Fundamentalism." Thus, Christopher Connelly titled his lead review of *Infidels* in *Rolling Stone*: "Dylan Makes Another Stunning Comeback." For Connelly the new album sweeps away the problems of Dylan's Christian period. While the songs touch on religion (?) and politics, they are rooted "in an ineffably deep sadness: the sadness of broken hearts and broken dreams, the sadness of middle age, the sadness that has been the wellspring of great rock and roll from Robert Johnson to 'Every Breath You Take.' "[18]

The evidence seemed to be there, slickly packaged in the new album itself. The title, at first reading, was a far cry from earlier statements of faith. "Infidels" don't believe, do they? The

---

[17] Martin Keller, "Dylan Speaks," *Us* magazine, 2 Jan. 1984, p. 58.
[18] Christopher Connelly, "Dylan Makes Another Stunning Comeback," *Rolling Stone*, 24 Nov. 1983, p. 65.

songs, gripping and powerful, to be sure, were also parabolic, obscure, ridden with riddles. The cutting social protest continued, the flailing of greed and war, injustice, political deception—the darkness of human nature and the final night descending upon us all. But what answers did Dylan now offer? Only the all-too-human whimper: "Don't fall apart on me tonight/I don't think I can handle it." Here Dylan demands what he himself cannot give, and the curtain drops.

Any spirituality, it was supposed, was to be found in the warnings against being deceived by a false spirituality and a defense of Zionism (in "Neighborhood Bully"). For those convinced that Dylan had returned to Judaism, what better evidence could there be than that of the record sleeve picture of Dylan in Israel with the old city of Jerusalem shimmering behind him?

Infidels clearly struck a chord. Greeted by rave reviews, it raced up the charts and within weeks was in the number four position passing Culture Club's *Colour by Numbers* and the Rolling Stones' *Under Cover*. Shortly thereafter it went gold. As the reviews came in, prognosticators concluded that Dylan had again zigzagged out of harm's way. With his career stagnant, his recent albums angrily received, and his fans in disarray, Dylan had made a spectacular end run around the opposition by abandoning his "born-again stance" and appealing to the disillusionment and despair of the age. To be sure, such suggestions are tinged with cynicism—is Dylan basically captive to keeping his career alive? All the same, the idol and superstar seemed safely back in the fold, the perplexing and embarrassing Christian era now ended.

It is the contention of this book that the above thesis, while plausible, is wrong and that the generalizations about *Infidels* are vastly oversimplified and one-sided. This is due to wishful thinking, on the one hand, and the ignorance of Dylan's thought and direction in his previous three albums of the Slow Train Era, on the other. In fact, the songs on *Infidels* are rooted not in Connelly's "ineffably deep sadness," but in Dylan's prophetic sense of where history is right now. As we shall see later, both in *Infidels* and in current interviews, Dylan has littered the landscape with clues and confessions as to his present spiritual state. While speculation over the genuineness and enduring nature of Dylan's

23

Christian conversion continues to run wild, what are the facts? Dylan writes in "Saving Grace":

> The wicked know no peace
> And you just can't fake it
> There's only one road
> And it leads to Calvary.
>
> (on *Saved*)

What caused Dylan to take that road? How certain was and is his journey? To this we now turn.

Chapter 2—Odyssey

*"There's a dying voice within me
Reaching out somewhere. . . ."*

©1984 Los Angeles Times/Patrick Downs

DYLAN WRITES IN "Love Minus Zero/No Limit" that "there's no success like failure." This irony became true in Dylan's journey to Christianity which was marked by two decades of unprecedented success—and failure. As he created and reflected the culture of the sixties and seventies, which by any measure was a historical watershed, he ran through and out of his options. Dylan experienced several overlapping stages in the process, adopting the successive roles of political activist, anarchic, druggy mystic, moralistic preacher, and incurable romantic. The continuity through all of this was, as he told Robert Hilburn of the *Los Angeles Times*, ". . . just to . . . get down to the root reality of the way things really are, to pull the mask off. My thing was always to pull the mask off of whatever was going on." As Dylan pulled off the masks, so the masks were pulled off him. Again he tells Hilburn, "I had gone so far that I didn't even think there was anything left. I thought, 'Well, everybody has got their own truth.' What works for one man is fine as long as it works for him. I had given up looking and searching for it."[1]

Dylan described his pulling off of the masks in "Every Grain of Sand" on *Shot of Love*. Here he takes the listener on a relentless trek through his past which climaxes in a radical conversion. As the darkness descends on his terminal agony, Dylan speaks of a "dying voice within me reaching out somewhere. . . ." It is our intention to listen to that "dying voice" as we review his journey to Christ.

We begin then with "the Movement," the rush of political

---

[1] Robert Hilburn, "Dylan: 'I Learned That Jesus Is Real and I Wanted That,' " *Los Angeles Times*, 23 Nov. 1980, Calendar, p. 8.

protest in the early sixties that was to send a generation into the streets, break the back of institutional racism and the Vietnam War, and catapult Dylan into the public eye. Political problems demand political solutions. Dylan became, for a season, the champion of this naive but enduring assumption.

The Political Mask

In "Every Grain of Sand" Dylan describes "The violence of a summer's dream/In the chill of a wintery light." The "summer's dream" in 1961 was the liberation of black America from a hundred years of "slave mentality." The "chill of a wintery light" was the pride and prejudice of unending egoism which would shatter that dream.

Martin Luther King stood before the masses at the Lincoln Memorial and saw the Promised Land. In his rich rolling cadence, like a black Moses looking across Jordan, he intoned, "I have a dream. . . ." The dream had ignited a generation of college students, sending them South to register voters, ride buses, picket, and end, once and for all, the stigma of segregation. Their ideology was Gandhi's nonviolence. They marched arm in arm and sang in the streets, "We shall overcome someday." Now, at last, they would be the generation to fulfill the American millennium: equality in the context of material plenty and military security. They lived in the glow of John F. Kennedy's Camelot. They had answered his call to do something for their country.

Dotson Rader, a young activist, expresses the idealistic hopes of many at that time. He writes, "When my religious faith petered out . . . my faith in the Dream of the country grew. America-To-Come became vital. Without any . . . Foursquare City to prepare for, with no Second Coming to establish the City of God, I had to work to end the mess. I was responsible." Social change became Rader's religion. He admits, "Many of us (like Tom Haden, cofounder of SDS, raised in a Catholic home) were believers without a faith in need of Mission. Only that—the assurance of Mission—provided meaning."[2]

---

[2] Dotson Rader, *I Ain't Marching Anymore* (New York: Paperback Library, 1969), pp. 12-13.

The music of protest was folk. Rooted in America's past, it was "message music." Woody Guthrie, the Depression drifter, political radical, and people's poet, had written "This Land Is Your Land," but it was balding Pete Seeger with the Weavers who brought his message to electrified campus audiences. Buttondown collars gave way to blue jeans and bib-overalls. No designer labels compromised this generation's identification with the working poor.

Next came Joan Baez with her raven black hair and chiseled features, singing traditional ballads in a clear, bell-like voice. She stirred the consciences of the Ivy League circuit along with Peter, Paul, and Mary, a captivating, enormously popular trio. The market, however, was ripe for a new generation of protest songs that would speak to the mounting crisis rather than simply recall past injustices. The troubadours were looking for new material, and the students were ready to hear it. At this apocalyptic moment, Bob Dylan, the Jewish boy from Hibbing, Minnesota, arrived in Greenwich Village via Minneapolis, lugging his acoustical guitar and knapsack, and stepped into history.

In quick order, the frail, scruffy Dylan was befriended by the folk music world, landed a recording contract with Columbia, picked up a manager in Albert Grossman, and surfaced as Joan Baez's unannounced guest at her concerts. Playing around the folk circuit, Dylan built a following among students, received media attention, and began to pummel his audiences with biting lyrics and simple, memorable tunes. As the vacuum for new folk music was being filled by Dylan, the stage was also being set for his launch into fame before an aroused, angry, idealistic public. It all came together for Dylan with one song, "Blowin' in the Wind," and in one setting—the 1963 Newport Folk Festival.

Anthony Scaduto calls the Newport Folk Festival "literally Dylan's crowning moment."[3] There, before 46,000 people, gathered for three days of traditional and protest music, Dylan was transformed from a "hobo minstrel" into "the electric poet-visionary-hero who was orchestrating a 'youth revolution.'" Scaduto described Dylan as looking "thinner and more under-nourished, more ascetic and pained than ever before. . . . He

---

[3] Anthony Scaduto, *Bob Dylan* (New York: New American Library, 1973), p. 172.

generated visions of a young man on a death trip: rebellious, living fast and dangerously. . . ." Even before Dylan stepped on the stage, the mention of his name brought cheers. When he finally appeared, it was to a stunning ovation. Scaduto reports that when Dylan started to sing "Blowin' in the Wind," Joan Baez spontaneously joined him, her "clear soprano flowing behind and above and around his harsh nasal voice, and all those on stage rose from their chairs and celebrated his triumph with him: Seeger, Bikel, Peter, Paul, and Mary, and the Freedom Singers, harmonizing Dylan's song." The crowd roared for more, and the performers, moved by the unprecedented ovation, improvised a finale by "locking hands, swaying from side to side, singing *We Shall Overcome*." Scaduto concludes that for those who had never heard Dylan before, his impact was overwhelming. "They had come to take part in a movement and they discovered a prophet." Later, Joan Baez was to describe Dylan in "Diamonds and Rust":

> Well, you burst on the scene
> Already a legend
> The unwashed phenomenon
> The original vagabond
> You strayed into my arms.

If Baez was the queen of folk music, Dylan was the crown prince who would soon take his throne.

There is no need for us to review Dylan's torrent of "finger-pointin' " songs that critiqued racism, the Cuban missile crisis, and the darkening shadow of Vietnam. His values are humanistic. His outrage is based on a stern morality. In "Masters of War" he sees the business behind the bombs, "I just want you to know/I can see through your masks" (on *The Freewheelin' Bob Dylan*). And he does it with metered rage and simplistic accuracy.

But why was political activism also a mask for Bob Dylan? Why was it a "summer's dream" in the "chill of a wintery light" ("Every Grain of Sand" on *Shot of Love*)? In the first place, Dylan was too smart to be the prisoner of any particular cause. As he told Nat Hentoff, "I looked around and saw all these people pointing fingers at the bomb. But the bomb is getting boring, because what's wrong goes much deeper than the bomb. What's wrong is how few people are free. . . . I mean, they have some kind of vested interest in the way things are now."[4] When Dylan was given the Tom Paine Award from the Emergency Civil Liberties Committee in December 1963, he made his point publicly. The setting was a dinner at the Americana Hotel in New York City. Tempers flared as Dylan, before a glittering, monied crowd of liberal activists, identified himself not with John Kennedy, but with Kennedy's killer, Lee Harvey Oswald. Dylan had been uptight like Oswald. Then Dylan went on to speak of junkies in Harlem and asked what anyone was doing for their freedom. By then the chairman was kicking Dylan under the table and boos were filling the hall. Dylan recalled, "Those people at that dinner were the same as everybody else. They're doing their time. They're trying to put morals and great deeds on their chains, but basically . . . they got their jobs to keep."[5] In other words, northern liberals and southern blacks alike are in bondage. Political acts are all self-serving and only rearrange the deck chairs on the Titanic. Later, Dylan put it succinctly in his protest song about the murdered Black Panther leader, "George Jackson":

> Sometimes I think this whole world
> Is one big prison-yard
> Some of us are prisoners
> The rest of us are guards.

However, if the world is one big prison yard, then moral judgments become more difficult to make. Who wears the white hats and who wears the black hats? In "My Back Pages" Dylan rejects his morals of protest with the bitter irony of hating hatred:

> Half-wracked prejudice leaped forth
> 'Rip down all hate,' I screamed
> Lies that life is black and white
> Spoke from my skull. I dreamed. . . .
> (on *Another Side of Bob Dylan*)

---

[4] Nat Hentoff, "The Crackin', Shakin', Breakin' Sounds," in *Bob Dylan: A Retrospective*, ed. Craig McGregor (New York: William Morrow, 1972), p. 56.
[5] Ibid., p. 61.

With clear distinctions as lies, he is left in ambiguity: "Good and bad, I define these terms/Quite clear, no doubt, somehow."

But what about racism? Aren't blacks clearly subservient to the white majority? Again, Dylan goes beyond the obvious dichotomy, "Man, I just don't see any colors at all when I look out. . . . There's no black and white, left and right, to me anymore. There's only up and down and down is very close to the ground. And I'm trying to go up without thinking of anything trivial, such as politics."[6] If the world is a prison yard then the issue shifts to "up and down." It's no longer a political question. It's a spiritual question.

Not only did Dylan see through to the core of the political issue with its moral pretense, he also saw the immediate limitations of protest songs for his own art. In Nat Hentoff's *Playboy* (March 1966) interview, Dylan called political songs "already dead." He was right. Who today would be roused by a song about Emmett Till or Medgar Evers or even Martin Luther King? It is traditional music that is timeless. Dylan expounded, "It comes about from legends, Bibles, plagues, and it revolves around vegetables and death." For his own development Dylan was compelled to go beyond the folk idiom. In fact, he claimed to have used the protest movement to launch his own career. "I became interested in folk music because I had to make it somehow."[7] While this is true, it is only part of the truth. Dylan was not the mere opportunist he painted himself to be. He had a deep identification with Woody Guthrie (his last hero) and he cared about the people and the issues. When he went on in his own development, he took the folk influence with him.

The *"violence* of the summer's dream," however, was the optimism, idealism, and activism of the early sixties which collided with the "chill of a wintery light." As we have seen, that chill was not only the established, vested interests and the assassins' bullets felling Kennedy and King. The chill was ultimately the whole human dilemma, the chill of the human heart.

Pulling off the political mask, Dylan now turned inward. His alternative was to find the freedom he sought, not in "The Move-

---

[6] Scaduto, *Bob Dylan*, p. 189.
[7] Nora Ephron and Susan Edmiston, "Bob Dylan Interview," in *Bob Dylan: A Retrospective*, p. 85.

ment" but within himself. As he told Nat Hentoff, "From now on, I want to write from inside me, and to do that I'm going to have to get back to writing like I used to when I was ten—having everything come out naturally."[8] By leaving politics behind, Dylan was in advance of his generation by several years. His closest friends were to malign him for "giving up" on their agendas. With prophetic vision, however, Dylan saw the superficiality of the political mask he had worn. His world offered another alternative—the inner space of the self, the hallucinogenic high, leading either to peace or madness. Would the collapse of the external political order result in a collapse of the internal psychological order as well? Would the quest for self-fulfillment lead to self-destruction? In this, Dylan was to anticipate where the culture of the seventies would go, ending up in a mania of narcissism.

The Anarchic/Druggy/Mystical Mask

In "Every Grain of Sand" Dylan writes:

> There's a dying voice within me
> Reaching out somewhere
> Toiling in the danger
> And in the morals of despair.

It was the "danger" and the "morals of despair" that began to grip more and more of those who gave up on the idealism of the protest movement. In rage many blacks turned to violence. The Panthers were born and the ghettos burned in the hot summer months. As Vietnam preoccupied the nation, so the resistance intensified: "Hell, no, we won't go!" With the critique of the "technological society," the student generation looked for an alternative, a counterculture. Psychedelic drugs and their high priest, Timothy Leary ("turn on, tune in, drop out"), seemed to open up a new world. Eastern mysticism flooded into the spiritual vacuum, and all of this was marketed through stereophonic sound by the cultural high priests—the pop musicians.

Dylan, in turning to electric music, in recovering his rock

---

[8] Hentoff, "The Crackin', Shakin', Breakin' Sounds," in *Bob Dylan: A Retrospective,* p. 47.

roots, and in abandoning the protest movement was well in advance of the pack. It was he who recreated the American music scene with "folk rock." Seeking personal freedom, Dylan also explored the possibilities of drugs and their mystical consequences: he trafficked in the "morals of despair." Moreover, Dylan now became a superstar in his own right.

At the Newport Folk Festival in 1965 Dylan went electric and, in Paul Nelson's words, "provided . . . the most dramatic scene I've ever witnessed in folk music."[9] Dylan walked on the stage carrying an electric guitar. Backed up by the Paul Butterfield Blues Band, he shocked the folk crowd with his new music and was driven off after a few numbers by the roar of hecklers' boos. Some reported that there were tears in his eyes. There were certainly tears in the eyes of folk patriarch Pete Seeger who, as Scaduto narrates it, "was standing off to one side while rock was desecrating the hallowed Folk Festival ground."[10] After Peter Yarrow pled with the audience to clap for Dylan to return, he did come back to sing, "It's All Over Now, Baby Blue." It was "all over" for the folk crowd, and it was "all over" for Bob Dylan with them, too.

Nelson sees a great historical divide represented by Pete Seeger and Bob Dylan at this festival. He writes of Dylan, ". . . like some fierce young Spanish outlaw in dress leather jacket, a man who could no longer accept the older singer's vague humanistic generalities, a man who, like Nathanael West, had his own angry vision to project. . . ."[11] The idealistic veneer of ethical demand based upon the liberal assumption of humanitarian "goodwill" no longer worked. The angry vision of human darkness would now dominate Dylan.

In the spring of that year, Dylan had projected an angry vision indeed with the release of his album *Bringing It All Back Home*. Here he showed the absurdity of middle-class expectations in "Subterranean Homesick Blues." In this "talking blues" with its clipped verses he warns about responsibility: "Look out, kid/It's somethin' you did." But then who cares about responsibility anyway? "Look out, kid/You're gonna get hit." Is life ab-

---

[9] Paul Nelson, "Newport Folk Festival, 1965," in *Bob Dylan: A Retrospective*, p. 73.
[10] Scaduto, *Bob Dylan*, p. 246.
[11] Nelson, "Newport Folk Festival, 1965," in *Bob Dylan: A Retrospective*, p. 75.

surd? You bet. It's been vandalized: "Look out, kid/They keep it all hid. . . . The pump don't work/'Cause the vandals took the handles." In the same song Dylan issues his famous warning: "Don't follow leaders/Watch the parkin' meters." Here he has clearly left his protest period and his old self far behind. For Ralph Gleason, Dylan portrayed ". . . the growing realization of the surrealism of our real world."[12] One contribution to this was his involvement in drugs.

It is clear that drugs played an important role for Dylan at this time. Scaduto interviews a close woman friend of Dylan's who quotes him as saying, "I'm pro-chemistry." She continues, "After he got into the drugs he stopped denying that thing inside himself. He began looking for it, believing in it, working with it and letting it flow over him. The drugs got him back to that mystic inner self."[13] Later, in speaking to Nat Hentoff about drugs, Dylan said, "But opium and hash and pot—now, those things aren't drugs; they just bend your mind a little. I think *everybody's* mind should be bent once in a while. Not by LSD, though. LSD is medicine—a different kind of medicine. It makes you aware of the universe so to speak; you realize how foolish objects are. . . ."[14]

Dylan's memorable song about drugs is his classic "Mr. Tambourine Man," on *Bringing It All Back Home*. First he calls upon his muse, "Take me on a trip upon your magic swirlin' ship." Then he writes:

> I'm ready to go anywhere, I'm ready for to fade
> Into my own parade, cast your dancing spell my way,
> I promise to go under it.

And he continues, "Then take me disappearin' through the smoke rings of my mind." But it is not for some transcendent experience that Dylan prays. He simply wants to "forget about today until tomorrow"; a clear commentary on "the morals of despair."

Years later Dylan would write in "Every Grain of Sand":

[12] Ralph Gleason, "The Children's Crusade," in *Bob Dylan: A Retrospective*, p. 178.
[13] Scaduto, *Bob Dylan*, pp. 181-182.
[14] Nat Hentoff, "The Playboy Interview: Bob Dylan," in *Bob Dylan: A Retrospective*, p. 141.

I have gone from rags to riches
And the sorrow of the night
. . . . .

And the bitter dance of loneliness
Fading into space
And the broken mirror of innocence
On each forgotten face.

"The bitter dance of loneliness/Fading into space" can be viewed as Dylan's judgment on his druggy past. This is especially true when he asks "Mr. Tambourine Man" to "cast your dancing spell my way" and dances "beneath the diamond sky with one hand waving free."

But the dance is *bitter* because it's lonely. The drugs drive him into himself. He escapes into his "own parade." It's also bitter because it's fading. There's always the "morning after."

Here, then, are two aspects of "toiling in the danger and in the morals of despair." Dylan sees the absurdity of life and deals with it by tripping out. Even at this point, however, there is another side to Bob Dylan—the mystic vision.

Dylan offered resolution for all the chaos he felt in "Gates of Eden," also on *Bringing It All Back Home*. It's in Eden that false religious promises are laughed at. It's in Eden that "relationships of ownership" and "succeeding kings" no longer exist. It's in Eden that the discussion of reality no longer matters. It's in Eden that dreams are the words to tell what's true, "and there are no truths outside the Gates of Eden." But this Eden is not the biblical heaven where God is loved and praised, for "no sound ever comes from the Gates of Eden." Eden is a dream of silence. A mystic trance. As Ellen Willis puts it, psychedelic music "focused on the trip—especially the flight—the way folk music focused on the road."[15]

For Dylan, however, drugs became a dead end. In 1969 he reflected on those earlier days: "I was on the road for almost five years. It wore me down. I was on drugs, a lot of things. A lot of things just to keep me going, you know?"[16] In a previous interview Dylan concluded, "I wouldn't think they [drugs] have anything to offer. . . . From my own experience they would have

---

[15] Ellen Willis, "Dylan," in *Bob Dylan: A Retrospective*, p. 232.
[16] Jann Wenner, "The Rolling Stone Interview," in *Bob Dylan: A Retrospective*, p. 320.

nothing positive to offer."[17] Drugs may lead to mysticism, but they may also lead to madness. If the world outside is chaotic and confusing, the world inside becomes the same. On the liner notes to *Bringing It All Back Home* Dylan writes, "i accept chaos. i am not sure whether it accepts me." But as Nietzsche warns, "Look not too long into the abyss, lest the abyss looks into thee." And the abyss was looking into Dylan.

On *Highway 61 Revisited*, released in 1965 just after the Newport Folk Festival, Dylan cut one of his most honored rockers, "Like a Rolling Stone." In it he expresses profound lostness. The chorus reads:

> How does it feel?
> How does it feel?
> To be without a home
> Like a complete unknown
> Like a rolling stone?

On one level, Dylan may be asking this of a former friend. On another level Dylan may be asking this of himself. And on still another level this may be asked of the whole generation of the sixties (and the seventies and eighties). In the remaining choruses the line "To be without a home" is changed to "To be on your own/With no direction home." The drug trip, the mystical flight simply ends up in alienation, in cosmic loneliness, in the "morals of despair." And for many, there was no way back. This is why it is a dead end.

The mystic's quest for oneness with all things, often generated by hallucinogenic drugs, is, as Dietrich Bonhoeffer says, "the soul chattering to itself." It is the ultimate idolatry, to be unconsciously alone in a state of bliss and claim that state to be all there is, or even God Himself (or Itself!).

Moreover, such mysticism is amoral. For it, either evil is illusion, or good and evil coexist in some harmonious, yin–yang balance. Again, Dylan cared too much and saw too much to accept that kind of escapism. Whether he is putting down the reporter who doesn't understand in "Ballad of a Thin Man" or indicting the entire culture in "Desolation Row," Dylan con-

---

[17] John Cohen and Happy Traum, "Conversations With Bob Dylan," in *Bob Dylan: A Retrospective*, pp. 288–289.

Bob Dylan and Joan Baez join together once again to sing at Peace Sunday at the Rose Bowl in June 1982.

tinues his protest against the world as it is. Here is his tension. He is unable to flee into his "own parade" or get lost in the gates of Eden. The "morals of despair" are simply not enough, but, unlike his protest period, now he can provide no answers. Dylan's critique of the culture and his surrealistic visions climax in his next album, *Blonde on Blonde*. There is something new here too—the awesome power of romantic love.

For Alan Rinzler, this double album released in 1966, ". . . marks the apex of Dylan's career as a rock 'n' roll star."[18] Dylan is racing. In "Rainy Day Women #12 and 35" he tells us, "Everybody must get stoned." The lighthearted music and heavy-handed lyrics punch home the irony of getting stoned: Rejection is the universal condition and escape is the universal possibility.

Dylan's nightmare vision of our lives, the "Desolation Row" where we all live, surfaces in "Stuck Inside of Mobile With the Memphis Blues Again." Here is the congenial hell of Sartre's *No Exit*, where the pain is soothed: "Ladies treat me kindly." It is still hell, however, for ". . . deep in my heart/I know I can't escape." It is also a Kafkaesque place where no messages can be sent, for ". . . the post office has been stolen/And the mailbox is locked."

In this world Dylan sees the impotence of the structures we have staked our lives upon. The family, government, organized religion—all have failed. As far as the family goes, Grandpa went crazy and died. And government? The senator, using his own children for votes, hands out free tickets for his son's wedding. Of course, Dylan didn't get one—he's on the outside. What, then, about religion? Rather than delivering God's Word, the preacher hid behind social causes to effect relevance, "With twenty pounds of headlines/Stapled to his chest." To be sure, he isn't happy when Dylan sees through him.

> But he cursed me when I proved to him,
> Then I whispered, 'Not even you can hide
> You see, you're just like me
> I hope you're satisfied.'

---

[18] Alan Rinzler, *Bob Dylan: The Illustrated Record* (New York: Harmony Books, 1978), p. 55.

With this collapse of order, can Dylan "blow it all off" by escaping into drugs? The "rainman," a dealer, offers two cures for this theater of the absurd. Foolishly, Dylan mixes them.

> An' it strangled up my mind
> An' now people just get uglier
> An' I have no sense of time.

Some cure!

Maybe a woman can deliver him from this mess. For "Ruthie," however, love is seduction. When Dylan tells her about his debutante, she replies, "Your debutante just knows what you need/But I know what you want."

Dylan's "Memphis Blues" ends in hopelessness (and a slam at reincarnation).

> An' here I sit so patiently
> Waiting to find out what price
> You have to pay to get out of
> Going through all these things twice.

Nevertheless, as we have suggested, Dylan takes a step beyond the "morals of despair" and his druggy, mystical mask in *Blonde on Blonde.* What will deliver him from the cynicism of failed protest, the madness of anarchy, and the mindlessness of drug-mysticism? Could it be a woman? Is life to be found in relationships, after all? Dylan's love songs reveal the direction in which he is moving.

In this album Dylan goes through the full range of his emotions with women. He expresses remorse in "One of Us Must Know (Sooner or Later)," the put-down in "Just Like a Woman," tentative hope in "Pledging My Time," and haunting memory in "Visions of Johanna." In retrospect, one song, "Sad-Eyed Lady of the Lowlands," becomes significant for the future. Years later, Dylan writes to his wife Sara:

> I can still hear the sounds
> Of those Methodist bells
> I'd taken the cure
> And had just gotten through

Stayin' up for days
In the Chelsea Hotel
Writin' 'Sad-Eyed Lady
Of the Lowlands' for you.
("Sara" on *Desire*)

The "Sad-Eyed Lady" whom he describes takes on a spiritual quality that has not appeared before in Dylan's songs. He begins:

With your mercury mouth in the missionary times
And your eyes like smoke and your prayers like rhymes.
And your silver cross, and your voice like chimes
Oh, who among them do they think could bury you?

A religious aura hovers over this lady, and she is immortal. At the end of the song again Dylan writes:

With your holy medallion which your fingertips fold.
And your saintlike face and your ghostlike soul,
Oh, who among them do you think could destroy you?

Dylan wrote to Ralph Gleason in 1965, "i've conceded the fact there is no understanding of anything. at best, just winks of the eye an' that is all i'm lookin' for now i guess."[19] Can, however, a woman relieve him from "Toiling in the danger/And in the morals of despair"? Can she interrupt "The bitter dance of loneliness/Fading into space"? Yes and no.

Bob Dylan and Sara Lowndes were married in November 1965. Then Dylan went on tour for six months. After his return he had a near-fatal accident, crashing his motorcycle in the summer of 1966. His marriage followed by his accident dramatically altered his life. Fast on the way to becoming the nation's next Elvis Presley, Dylan was knocked out of his life in the fast lane. He simply vanished. The mask of the druggy, superstar, rock 'n' roll king lay in the twisted metal of his bike on a road near Woodstock, New York. Stopped dead in his tracks, Dylan was forced to rebuild his life and to build his marriage. There was much to be renewed.

---

[19] Gleason, "The Children's Crusade," in *Bob Dylan: A Retrospective*, p. 183.

The Moral/Religious/Romantic Mask

As Dylan recovered from his accident, he also recovered his roots. This springtime of moral and spiritual regeneration, however, was to prove ephemeral. As the flowers grow, so the weeds grow. Thus, in "Every Grain of Sand," Dylan writes:

> Oh, the flowers of the mountains
> And the weeds of yester-year
> Like criminals they have choked the breath
> Of conscience and good cheer.

With conscience and good cheer gone, all that is left is the remembrance of what has been lost. Dylan continues:

> Oh, the sun beat down upon the steps
> Of time to light the way
> To ease the pain of idleness
> And the memory of decay.
>
> (on *Shot of Love*)

For the present, however, Dylan was alive again. If there is a God, if there is a transcendent reality beyond time and space, then there may also be a divine order for life. In his Jewish-biblical roots, Dylan searched out that moral order.

With his next album, *John Wesley Harding*, Dylan turned country and western and took much of pop music with him. If he was looking for his roots, this was the ideal genre. Anthony Scaduto comments, "*John Wesley Harding* is infused with a belief in God, with self-discovery and compassion. It is Dylan's version of the Bible, songs written as parables describing the fall and rebirth of one man—Bob Dylan."[20]

Dylan himself, however, denied this. He told Happy Traum, "I'm not in the songs anymore. . . . I'm not personally connected with them."[21] This was probably an overstatement, but the truth is that here Dylan crafts his poetry before going into the studio to record. His use of the acoustical guitar also evidences his return to simplicity. Several songs now end with a moral. In this

---

[20] Scaduto, *Bob Dylan*, p. 286.
[21] Cohen and Traum, "Conversations With Bob Dylan," in *Bob Dylan: A Retrospective*, p. 280.

album, Jon Landau asserts, Dylan puts on the new mask of "the moderate man," the "adult Dylan."[22] Reflecting back, Dylan tells Jonathan Cott, "*John Wesley Harding* was a fearful album—just dealing with fear (laughing), but dealing with the devil in a fearful way, almost."[23]

Dylan sets his theme, in a major song on the album, "All Along the Watchtower." The moment is apocalyptic with a growling wildcat, the howling wind, and unknown riders approaching from a distance. In this setting, a joker and a thief converse. The joker complains of his confusion (the "morals of despair"?) and the thief responds:

> 'No reason to get excited,' the thief he kindly spoke
> 'There are many here among us who feel that life is but a joke.
> But you and I, we've been through that, and this is not our fate.
> So let us not talk falsely now, the hour is getting late.'

Here Dylan no longer accepts the absurdity of life. It is no joke. Furthermore, in the lateness of the hour, it is a time for truth.

The truth comes in moralizing ballads about a Robin Hood bandit, "John Wesley Harding," and the danger of confusing Paradise with fleshly pleasures in "The Ballad of Frankie Lee and Judas Priest."

The truth comes in visions, such as in "I Dreamed I Saw St. Augustine" where Dylan shares responsibility for the martyrdom of this Christ-figure. He writes:

> And I dreamed I was amongst the ones
> That put him out to death
> Oh, I awoke in anger
> So alone and terrified,
> I put my fingers against the glass
> And bowed my head and cried.

The truth comes by divine intervention in "Drifter's Escape," when a vagrant is delivered from the "cursed jury" and the crowd outside the courtroom.

---

[22] Jon Landau, "John Wesley Harding," in *Bob Dylan: A Retrospective*, p. 259.
[23] Jonathan Cott, "Bob Dylan, 1978," in *The Rolling Stone Interviews* (New York: St. Martin's Press/Rolling Stone Press, 1981), p. 359.

> Just then a bolt of lightning
> Struck the courthouse out of shape,
> And while everybody knelt to pray
> The drifter did escape.

The truth also comes in exposing "The Wicked Messenger," a satanic figure whose tongue "could not speak, but only flatter." In the final stanza he is told by the crowd, "If ye cannot bring good news, then don't bring any." This is certainly a dramatic reversal from the chaotic, cynical Dylan of "Desolation Row" and "Memphis Blues." A new spirituality has surfaced.

Two albums later and Dylan is actually writing prayers. In "Father of Night," on *New Morning*, he offers a psalm to the Creator who "dwells in our hearts and our memories." He is:

> Father of night, Father of day
> Father, who taketh the darkness away.

On the same album in "Three Angels," while the common drudgery of life goes on below, the angelic statues play their horns. Dylan concludes:

> The angels play on their horns all day,
> The whole earth in progression seems to pass by.
> But does anyone hear the music they play,
> Does anyone even try?

Certainly Dylan is trying. In the words of a song he wrote for the movie *Pat Garrett and Billy the Kid*, he's "Knock, knock, knockin' on heaven's door."

Dylan's spritual quest in this period included several trips to Israel. He even considered moving his family to a kibbutz for a year, but his star status made him vulnerable to being used by organized religion and he backed off.

If it was Dylan's renewed faith in God that gave him order in the midst of chaos and a transcendental ground for morality, it was love that made life worth living.

There is an ambivalence throughout Dylan's poetry on romantic love. On the one hand there are those women who represent the ideal in body and spirit. There is "The Girl of the North

Country," "a true love of mine" (on *The Freewheelin' Bob Dylan*); there are the "Visions of Johanna" "that conquer my mind," and there is the "Sad-Eyed Lady of the Lowlands," with her "saint-like face and . . . ghostlike soul" (on *Blonde on Blonde*).

On the other hand, there is the selfish, possessive, demanding love in "It Ain't Me, Babe" (on *Another Side of Bob Dylan*). Dylan sums up this love in "Don't Think Twice, It's All Right":

> I once loved a woman, a child I'm told
> I gave her my heart but she wanted my soul.
> (on *The Freewheelin' Bob Dylan*)

In these songs Dylan is "movin' on."

Nevertheless, Dylan found in his love for Sara the meaning of life. As he puts it in "I Threw It All Away" on *Nashville Skyline:*

> Love is all there is, it makes the world go 'round,
> Love and only love, it can't be denied.
> No matter what you think about it
> You just won't be able to do without it
> Take a tip from one who's tried.

Dylan stands in awe of Sara's love. Again and again he uses religious language to describe his relationship with her. As God created Adam by breathing into him the breath of life, so Sara does the same to Dylan. In his "Wedding Song" on *Planet Waves* he writes:

> You breathed on me and made my life
> A richer one to live.

Sara is also his savior, rescuing him from himself.

> When I was deep in poverty
> You taught me how to give.

Again, she has made sense of life. He writes:

> Without your love
> I'd be nowhere at all,
> I'd be lost if not for you,
> . . . .

45

> I just wouldn't have a clue
> Anyway it wouldn't ring true
> If not for you.
> ("If Not For You" on *New Morning*)

Thus, the sum total of life is wrapped up in her. As Dylan puts it in "Nobody 'Cept You":

> There's nothing here I believe in
> 'Cept you, yeah you
> And there's nothing to me that's sacred
> 'Cept you, yeah you.
> .   .   .
> Got nothing to live or die for
> 'Cept you, yeah you. . . .

What happens, then, when this relationship begins to crumble?

Dylan now reflects on the complexity of human love. His part mythical, part realistic epic poem of his life with Sara is titled "Tangled Up in Blue." It charts the union, separation, and reunion of two lovers. At the end of the song he writes:

> So now I'm goin' back again
> I got to get to her somehow
> .   .   .
> We always did feel the same
> We just saw it from a different point
> Of view
> Tangled up in blue.
> (on *Blood on the Tracks*)

In "Shelter From the Storm" on the same album he reveals:

> Now there's a wall between us
> Somethin' there's been lost
> I took too much for granted
> Got my signals crossed.

Perhaps the conclusion to Dylan's relationship with Sara and the failure of romantic love is given in "Idiot Wind" on *Blood on the Tracks*.

This whipping, crazy wind symbolizes the forces of chaos beyond Dylan's control. It blows through everything, bringing pain and ruin. The woman to whom he writes is an idiot, blown by the idiot wind. But in the last chorus, Dylan, too, is blown by the same wind.

> Idiot wind
> Blowing through the buttons of our coats
> Blowing through the letters that we wrote
> Idiot wind
> Blowing through the dust upon our shelves
> We're idiots, Babe
> It's a wonder we can even feed ourselves.

What was it that finally destroyed their union? Dylan writes of outside forces:

> It was gravity which pulled us down
> And destiny which broke us apart,

but the ultimate cause lies in himself.

> You tamed the lion in my cage
> But it just wasn't enough to change my heart.

Dylan's moral and religious renewal came together in the crisis of his near-fatal accident and in his marriage to Sara Lowndes. He gave Sara an ultimate devotion and gratitude which in its lyrical expression verges on worship. After the collapse of this center for his life there was nothing. He anticipated this in "Shelter From the Storm" when he wrote, ". . . nothing really matters much/It's doom alone that counts." His more personal expression came in "Meet Me in the Morning":

> They say the darkest hour
> Is right before the dawn
> They say the darkest hour
> Is right before the dawn
> But you wouldn't know it by me
> Every day's been darkness since you been gone.
> (on *Blood on the Tracks*)

The religious mask of devotion, the moral mask of order, the romantic mask of ecstasy were all gone. Again, as Dylan puts it in "Every Grain of Sand":

> Oh, the flowers of the mountains
> And the weeds of yester-year
> Like criminals they have choked the breath
> Of conscience and good cheer.

Now there is only "the pain of idleness/and the memory of decay." "It's doom alone that counts."

But this was not to be Dylan's bottom line. With his human options exhausted, there was one more possibility. As Martin Luther put it, "God creates out of nothing. You've got to be nothing for God to make something out of you."

The past stages of Dylan's life, both the flowers and weeds, must be surrendered. Again in "Every Grain of Sand," Dylan writes:

> Don't have the inclination
> To look back on any mistake
> Like Cain I now behold this
> Chain of events that I must break.

How then did Dylan break the "chain of events"? How did he really become a Christian? To this we now turn.

Chapter 3—Resolution

*"Surrender your crown
On this blood-stained ground
Take off your mask. . . ."*

©1984 Los Angeles Times/Patrick Downs

JANN WENNER, publisher of *Rolling Stone*, writes, "Dylan is the greatest singer of our times. No one is better. No one is even very close."[1] How then could this man, who both formed and represented so much of the rock world, become a Christian? Quickly it became necessary to explain Bob Dylan's conversion.

The Options

The critics asked: What moment of weakness? What personal crisis? What mental lapse brought Dylan to Christ? Since a psychological age demands (and provides) psychological explanations for everything, the reasons for Dylan's conversion seemed to be close at hand.

Even before Dylan's first concerts in San Francisco were over, Paul Williams was rushing *Dylan: What Happened?* into print, based on his historical sense of Dylan and the lyrics he heard at the Warfield Theater. Williams may have exploited Dylan in this hasty book, but he also displayed the anxiety among Dylan's fans to eliminate the personal threat of his conversion through some plausible explanation. Williams asks "What happened?" and answers his own question: "Well, in the very simplest terms, the divorce happened." He refers, of course, to Dylan's divorce from his wife Sara in 1977. Moving from what he holds to be this fixed point, Williams speculates that Dylan finally lost faith in the power of woman, and offers some cheap psychoanalysis: "He hadn't realized it at the time, but in freeing himself from Sara, he had, through great struggle, finally over-

---

[1] Jann Wenner, "Bob Dylan and Our Times: The Slow Train Is Coming," *Rolling Stone*, 20 Sept. 1979, p. 95.

come the power of all women over him—which meant also they could no longer help him ... he'd made himself immune." In place of woman, Dylan found "the uncritical hospitality of Jesus Christ."

The problem with this interpretation, however, is that Dylan had often expressed an ambivalence toward women. Deep relationships before Sara had been fractured without driving him to Christ. Also, Sara left in 1977, and Dylan did not become a Christian for over a year after that. He did not simply rebound into his new faith out of a pressing emotional crisis. Whatever the personal reasons, Williams must answer why Dylan turned to *Christ*.

Williams allows for "some kind of event outside his [Dylan's] control." But he then concludes that Dylan "found the discipline he needed to save himself in an American cultural ritual called giving oneself to Christ." This interpretation is strongly suspect for two reasons.

First of all, would the Dylan who had always run such a constant and penetrating critique of American life finally fall for "an American cultural ritual"? Anyone who knows Dylan knows that this conclusion is lame. In fact, his first Christian album, *Slow Train Coming*, continues (and recovers!) his devastating critique of American cultural rituals including religion. In the title song, "Slow Train," Dylan warns:

> But the enemy I see
> Wears a cloak of decency
> All non-believers and men-stealers
> Talkin' in the name of religion.

Dylan is hardly one to be captured by a religious ritual.

In the second place, Williams has failed to hear Dylan. He hasn't "saved himself," he has "been saved." The difference is decisive. Again on *Slow Train Coming*, in the song "Precious Angel," Dylan describes himself as "a little too blind to see," and then prays, "shine your light on me." That Dylan hasn't "saved himself" is crystal clear in the next album, *Saved*. Here, in the title song, he sings:

> I was blinded by the Devil
> Born already ruined

Stone-cold-dead
As I stepped out of the womb.

By His grace I have been touched
By His Word I have been healed
By His hand I've been delivered
By His Spirit I've been sealed.

I've been saved
By the blood of the Lamb. . . .

You can't have it both ways. Either you "save yourself" or you "have been saved." According to Dylan, he has *been saved*.

More judiciously, in *The Art of Bob Dylan*, Michael Gray pursues Paul Williams's thesis. The broader canvas is Dylan's yearning for salvation. Gray writes, "In fact the quest for salvation might well be called the central theme of Bob Dylan's entire output." For Gray, Dylan has always struggled with woman as his savior and the rejection of a woman's love "in the self-denial process necessary to his salvation." The early Dylan wrote "gotta-move-on" songs because a woman's love was not enough. Nevertheless, later, in the first blush of marriage, Dylan chooses a woman's love as his path to salvation. This, however, is inadequate, and so he tries to fuse God and woman in "Shelter From the Storm":

> If I could only turn back the clock
> To when God and her were born
> 'Come in,' she said 'I'll give you
> Shelter from the storm.'
> (on *Blood on the Tracks*)

Gray comments, that "the twists and turns . . . within Dylan's quest for salvation are . . . crucially connected with Dylan's own separation from, reconciliation with, and divorce from, his wife Sara." For him, this is the pivotal theme of all Dylan's major work of the seventies, "Dylan's journey is from Sara to Jesus."

Gray, however, pushes beyond Williams's failure/conversion scenario. Why, we must ask, did the shattering of Dylan's marriage bring him to Christ? Gray's answer is simple. In the process Dylan identified himself more and more with Christ. In fact, he actually confuses himself with Christ so that he becomes Christ. Both Christ and Dylan are betrayed; both are martyrs for their message. Gray concludes, "In retrospect, it is as if Dylan eventually converts to Christianity because of the way he has identified with Christ and understood His struggle through his own."[2]

Gray gives a more plausible explanation for Dylan's connection to Christ than Williams, but he too misses the point. For Dylan to so identify with Christ that he becomes Christ, is not to become a Christian. It is an act of consummate egotism. It is to replace Christ. Whatever previous tendency Dylan may have had in this direction has been abandoned in his conversion. Here in self-assertion Dylan does not become Christ, here in self-abasement Dylan is humbled before Christ. As he passionately sings in "When He Returns" on *Slow Train Coming:*

> The strongest wall
> Will crumble and fall
> To a mighty God
>
> For all those who have eyes
> And all those who have ears
> It is only He who can reduce me to tears

and

> Can I cast it aside
> All this loyalty and this pride
> Will I ever learn?

Then the call:

> Surrender your crown
> On this blood-stained ground
> Take off your mask.

These words are not written by a man becoming Christ. They are written by a man becoming a Christian.

---

[2] Michael Gray, *The Art of Bob Dylan* (New York: St. Martin's Press, 1981), p. 202. Michael Gross tries the same approach in *Bob Dylan: An Illustrated History* (New York: Tempo Books, 1980), but in a much more vulgar way, making a sexual interpretation, pp. 204-205.

Turning then from the attempts to explain Dylan's conversion, what are the facts? And especially what does Dylan say about them? This is more to the point.

Dylan's Journey

In the fall of 1978, Dylan was interviewed, while on tour, for *Rolling Stone* magazine by Jonathan Cott. Either during or soon after the tour Dylan was converted. Cott, however, reflected, "I had no clue that was happening."[3] Nevertheless, looking back at the interview, the clues are there.

For example, Cott asked Dylan about his doing new versions of his older songs. Dylan responded, "As I said before, the reason for the new versions is that I've changed. You meet new people in your life, you're involved on different levels with people. Love is a force, so when a force comes in your life—and there's love surrounding you—you can do anything." Cott asked, "Is that what's happening to you now?" Dylan replied, "Something similar to that, yeah." Later Cott returned to this theme: "I wanted to ask you about love." Dylan answered, "Go ahead, but I'm not too qualified on that subject. Love comes from the Lord—it keeps all of us going. If you want it, you got it."

Dylan also expressed the artist's experience of "inspiration" or "grace"; his art is a gift. He commented, "Woody Guthrie said he just picked songs out of the air. That meant that they were already there and that he was tuned into them."

Later, Dylan revealed a source of his connection to blacks and black music, to which we will return later. He recalled, "But when I was first living in New York City—do you remember the old Madison Square Garden? Well, they used to have gospel shows there every Sunday and you could see everyone from the Five Blind Boys, the Soul Stirrers and the Swan Silvertons to Clara Ward and the Mighty Clouds of Joy. I went up there every Sunday."

Near the end of the interview, Cott asked Dylan why he writes with so much complexity. Dylan, however, answered a broader question, "I wouldn't be doing it unless some power

[3] Jonathan Cott, "Bob Dylan, 1978," in *The Rolling Stone Interviews* (New York: St. Martin's Press/Rolling Stone Press, 1980), p. 354.

higher than myself were guiding me on. I wouldn't be here this long." If Dylan had not become a Christian by the time he gave this interview, it is clear that the hour was near.

In the course of this same tour, Dylan came to San Diego. During his concert someone threw a crucifix up on the stage. While he seldom picks things up, in this case he recalled, "I looked down at that cross and I said, 'I got to pick that up!'" Returning to San Diego the next year Dylan said to his audience, "If that person is here tonight, I want to thank you for that cross." The Slow Train for Bob Dylan was picking up speed.

It wasn't until November of 1980 that Dylan finally gave an interview in which he talked to Robert Hilburn of the *Los Angeles Times* about his conversion. Hilburn reports that Dylan "accepted Christ in his heart in 1978," but was reluctant initially to tell his friends about it or put his experience into music. Sitting in a hotel room in San Francisco, Dylan told Hilburn,

> The funny thing is a lot of people think that Jesus comes into a person's life only when they are either down or out or are miserable or just old and withering away. That's not the way it was for me. I was doing fine. [So much for Paul Williams and Michael Gray.] I had come a long way in just the year we were on the road (in 1978). I was relatively content, but a very close friend of mine mentioned a couple of things to me and one of them was Jesus.
>
> Well, the whole idea of Jesus was foreign to me. I said to myself, 'I can't deal with that. Maybe later.' But later it occurred to me that I trusted this person and I had nothing to do for the next couple of days so I called the person back and said I was willing to listen about Jesus.[4]

Dylan may be referring here to T-Bone Burnett, a lanky Texan who performed with Dylan's Rolling Thunder Review in 1975 and who influenced him toward Christ. Beyond Burnett, there was apparently also a woman who entered his life.

---

[4] Robert Hilburn, "Dylan: 'I Learned That Jesus Is Real and I Wanted That,'" *Los Angeles Times*, 23 Nov. 1980, Calendar, p. 1.

Four songs seem to speak of this special friend. On *Slow Train Coming*, Dylan writes in the title song of a woman in Alabama, a backwoods girl who "sure was realistic." He recalls:

> She said, 'Boy, without a doubt
> Have to quit your mess and straighten out
> You could die down here
> Be just another accident statistic.'

In "Gonna Change My Way of Thinking" on the same album, Dylan says he has a God-fearing woman whom he can easily afford: "She can do the Georgia Crawl/She can walk in the Spirit of the Lord." Likely she is also the woman described in "Precious Angel." She is the one who showed him he was blinded and gone, "How weak was the foundation/I was standing upon." Calling her "Precious Angel," Dylan promises her that no one can separate them from each other. They are both Christians, "We are covered in blood, girl" (the blood of Christ) and they share a common heritage. "You know both our forefathers were slaves." Certainly Dylan's Jewish forefathers were slaves in Egypt. But were her forefathers slaves in the South? This best explains a woman who does the Georgia Crawl and walks in the Spirit of the Lord. That Dylan is in love with her is also clear. She is both "Queen of my flesh" and "lamp of my soul." Thus, in her, the spiritual and sexual have authentically come together. On *Saved* Dylan sings to his "Covenant Woman." He promises to be faithful to her, trusts her, is grateful for her prayers, and sees her as a gift from God: "He must have loved me oh so much/To send me someone as fine as you."

The importance of this discussion is not just to connect historical clues; it reveals the "black" side of Dylan. The probability that Dylan was brought the gospel, in part, through a black woman shows a long line of continuity in his life which makes up a major part of his music. Anthony Scaduto writes that "Dylan was probably highly aware of color, for the black music experience had touched him deeply back in Hibbing (Minnesota), and the black experience had touched his very strong feelings for the oppressed. . . . In Hibbing and in Minneapolis he went out of his way to meet any black man connected with music; in New York he developed close friendships with a number of black men and women. *Friends*, not symbols."[5]

Dylan was deeply responsive to and influenced by soul music: blues and gospel. Behind rock 'n' roll lay the gospel beat and Dylan, as usual, had to get to the roots of it all. As we have seen, when he first arrived in New York City, he spent his Sunday afternoons listening to black gospel concerts. Later when Dylan drove across the country he stopped in New Orleans and visited the French Quarter, looking for music in the black bars. "That's where it's happening," he told his friends.[6]

It is also arguable that Dylan had special empathy for blacks because, as a Jew, he too felt on the outside of the Anglo-white middle-class culture. Throughout his career Dylan has written about the saga of blacks in America. He protests their murders in "The Death of Emmett Till," "Only a Pawn in Their Game," "The Lonesome Death of Hattie Carroll," and "George Jackson." He charges that Hurricane Carter, the black boxer, has been framed for a murder he didn't commit (in "Hurricane"). When he writes of the gangster "Joey" Gallo doing ten years in Attica State Prison he says:

> His closest friends were black men
> 'Cause they seemed to understand
> What it's like to be in society
> With a shackle on your hand.

Doesn't Dylan know that too, in his own way? Thus, when a black woman spoke to him about Christ he could hear what she said. This was not only because of an intimate friendship and the truth that she bore, but also because she came in the context of the black culture, which has contributed so much to his life.

Dylan was also introduced to two young pastors. He told Hilburn, "I was kind of skeptical, but I was also open. I certainly wasn't cynical. I asked lots of questions, questions like, 'What's the Son of God, what's all that mean?' and 'What does it mean—dying for my sins?' "[7]

---

[5] Anthony Scaduto, *Bob Dylan* (New York: New American Library, 1973), p. 172.
[6] Ibid., p. 196.
[7] Hilburn, "Dylan: 'I Learned That Jesus Is Real,' " p. 1.

By now Dylan is a pursued man. In "Every Grain of Sand" he describes this time. His eyes have been opened to see God, through creation.

> In the fury of the moment
> I can see the Master's hand
> In every leaf that trembles
> In every grain of sand.

Moreover, Dylan senses that the Divine Hand in creation also rests upon him.

> Then onward in my journey
> I come to understand
> That every hair is numbered
> Like every grain of sand.

Dylan is torn. Is it the living God? Is it his imagination? Graphically, he pictures the divided soul:

> I hear the Aged Footsteps
> Like the motion of the sea
> Sometimes, I turn, there's Someone there
> Othertimes, it's only me.

He is being pushed to the breaking point. It is the moment of truth. All that for which Dylan has searched, the very reality of his existence in the Reality of God is now before him. He concludes:

> I am hanging in the balance
> Of the "Reality of Man"
> Like every sparrow falling
> Like every grain of sand.
>   (on *Shot of Love*)

Arrival

Dylan told Robert Hilburn that he slowly began to accept that "Jesus is real and I wanted that . . . I knew that He wasn't going to come into my life and make it miserable, so one thing led to another . . . until I had this feeling, this *vision* and *feeling.*" Dylan reported that his room moved: "There was a presence in the room that couldn't have been anybody but Jesus."[8]

What happened in that moment? No one will ever fully know except Dylan, but several songs suggest aspects of that decisive hour in this rock star's life.

For Dylan, time stopped. It was like a slow, idyllic summer day. The moment had a sense of eternity around it. He writes:

> I was in your presence for an hour or so
> Or was it a day, I truly don't know
> Where the sun never set, where the trees hung low
> By that soft and shining sea.
>
> In the summertime, Ah—in the summertime
> In the summertime, when you were with me.
> ("In the Summertime" on *Shot of Love*)

Not only did Dylan experience that Divine Presence, he also experienced his own failure in a moment of final breaking. Dylan asks, "Did you respect me for what I did?" What he did was humble himself before Christ. He continues, "Or for what I didn't do/Or for keepin' it hid?" What he didn't do was save himself. He then asks, "Did I lose my mind/When I tried to get rid/Of everything you see?" Here is Dylan's radical break with his past, his "new birth." The threat of insanity lies in giving up the old life, the old identity, "everything you see." As Dietrich Bonhoeffer, the martyred German pastor, put it: "When Jesus calls a man He bids him come and die."

Thus, Dylan is both broken before Christ and made alive by Christ. In a startling image, as Dylan offers his heart to Christ for cleansing by His sacrificial blood, his clean (and empty) heart is also transfused by that same blood. It pumps through him as Christ becomes his life. He writes:

> I got the heart and you got the blood
> We cut through iron and we cut through mud.
> ("In the Summertime")

---

[8] Ibid., p. 8.

And what of the "iron" and "mud"? Was it the iron of his pride and the mud of his moral decay?

In this moment of transformation, Dylan clearly found release. More than once he speaks of his tears. On *Slow Train Coming* it is Christ alone "who can reduce me to tears" ("When He Returns"). These are the tears of repentance. But there are also tears that water hope.

> In the time of my confession
> In the hour of my deepest need
> When the pool of tears beneath my feet
> Floods every new-born seed.
> ("Every Grain of Sand" on *Shot of Love*)

And all of this is by the sheer grace of God. It is Christ who has done it all for Dylan, and who now meets him in his deepest need. As he puts it in "What Can I Do For You":

> You have given everything to me
> What can I do for you?
> . . . .
> Pulled me out of bondage
> And you made me renewed inside
> Filled up the hunger
> That had always been denied.
>
> Opened up a door no man can shut
> And you opened it up so wide
> And you've chosen me to be among the few
> What can I do for you?
> (on *Saved*)

It's difficult to describe this moment beyond Dylan's poetry without indulging in fantasy or becoming a spiritual voyeur. Even the bare bones, however, are incredible. Here is true drama.

Bob Dylan, part man, part myth, who "rocked the nation." Bob Dylan, creative genius, fantastically wealthy, commanding undreamed-of commercial success. Bob Dylan, fleeing the screams of rushing mobs, darting into escape limousines, hopping from coast to coast, continent to continent. Bob Dylan—the

man of many masks—the profile, the scraggly hair, the harmonica holder—drugs, women, adulation. Bob Dylan, hounded by the media, courted by the industry, his voice hourly on a thousand radio stations. Bob Dylan, picking songs out of the air to strip a generation of its idols as he fed its dreams. Bob Dylan—sexy, lithe, frail, brilliant, mysterious, arrogant, reclusive, sarcastic, tender, soaring from the depths to the heights.

Bob Dylan—at last—on his knees—an aching hunger—"broken, shattered like an empty cup." Bob Dylan alone in a room, "hanging in the balance."

But Bob Dylan now no longer alone, "in the fury of the moment"—the Ancient Footsteps—the Master's Hand. Bob Dylan weeping—a pool of tears. Bob Dylan bowing—a vision—a feeling—the presence of Jesus. Bob Dylan praying: "If you find it in your heart can I be forgiven . . ." ("Saving Grace" on *Saved*).

Dylan's conversion is Pauline; it is Augustinian. Like these classic Christians, he has an overwhelming sense of the sovereign call and grace of God, and it consumes him. He writes, "As I look around this world all that I'm seein'/Is the saving grace that is over me" ("Saving Grace").

Clearly, Dylan is not trafficking in some American ritual of self-salvation or in an egotistical identification of himself with Jesus. Neither is he, in Michael Gross's crass phrase, "giving Fundamentalism a whirl." Despite the prejudices of a psychological humanism and a closed "scientific" world view, Dylan has been met and transformed by the living Jesus Christ, who, because of His Resurrection from the dead is, in Sören Kierkegaard's phrase, "our contemporary."

Dylan, the Jewish outsider, partially through the friendship of a black woman, another outsider, came to Christ, the ultimate Outsider. But, here is the paradox: It is Christ, the Outsider, the Son of God who came from heaven to earth, who made Dylan an insider. Dylan found that the Creator is the Redeemer. In "What Can I Do for You" on *Saved*, Dylan writes, "You have explained every mystery." At last the contradictions are resolved. At last his heart is at rest. Pascal put it this way: "The knowledge of God without that of our wretchedness creates pride. The knowledge of our wretchedness without that of God creates despair. The knowledge of Jesus Christ is the middle way, because in him we find both God and our wretchedness."[9] Or as the Apostle Paul asserts, God made Christ "who knew no sin to be sin on our behalf, that we might become the righteousness of God in Him" (2 Corinthians 5:21 NAS). What then were the consequences of Dylan's conversion? To this we now turn.

The Consequences

The first result of Dylan's conversion was the impact of Christ on his personal life. Next, there was the question of his art. Finally, there was the issue of his friends and fans. Let us examine each of these briefly.

For Dylan personally there was a necessary period of quiet. As he explained to Robert Hilburn, "I truly had a born-again experience, if you want to call it that. It's an over-used term, but it's something that people can relate to. . . . I always knew there was a God or a creator of the universe and a creator of the mountains and the sea and all that kind of thing, but I wasn't conscious of Jesus and what that had to do with the supreme creator."[10] Having come to Christ, Dylan attended an intensive Bible study program for three months. He continued, "Most of the people I know don't believe that Jesus was resurrected, that He is alive. It's like He was just another prophet or something, one of many good people. That's not the way it was any longer for me. I had always read the Bible, but only looked at it as literature. I was never really instructed in it in a way that was meaningful to me."

Hilburn then asked if Dylan began to share his new faith. Dylan replied, "No, I didn't want to reflect on the Lord at all because if I told people and then I didn't keep going, they'd say, 'Oh well, I guess it was just another one of those things that didn't work out.' I didn't know myself if I could go for three months. But I did begin telling a few people after a couple of months and a lot of them got angry at me." Did this give Dylan second thoughts? "No, by that time, I was into it. When I believe in something, I don't care what anybody else thinks."

Next Hilburn asked Dylan if he feared that he wasn't really

---

[9] Blaise Pascal, *Pensées* (New York: The Modern Library, 1941).
[10] Hilburn, "Dylan: 'I Learned That Jesus Is Real,' " p. 8.

committed, that what he said now would haunt him in five years. Dylan replied, "I don't think so. If I would have felt anything like that, I think it would have come up to the surface by now [two years after his conversion]." Hilburn pressed his point: "But we've seen so many rock stars get involved with gurus and maharishis and then move on." Dylan responded, "Well, this is no maharishi trip with me. Jesus is definitely not that to me. . . . It's in my system."

As true as this is, it apparently did not keep Dylan from struggling with his faith. Thus, the media speculated about his possible lapse in early 1982. If Dylan hadn't struggled, however, he would be an unreal Christian. T-Bone Burnett, who originally influenced Dylan toward Christ, commented on the rumors: "As soon as someone, through some miracle, decides to change his life, all hell breaks loose. No matter what, people don't change just like that. It takes a lot of work to change—Christ's not like a magic wand. . . . To idolize a person is to murder him in a sense. You take away his humanity. People make mystical, pathological connections with their idols. Personally, I admire Dylan for having the guts to fail."[11]

With the release of *Infidels* Dylan granted another interview to Robert Hilburn in the fall of 1983. Hilburn asked him if he still considered himself "born again." Dylan answered by attacking the label: "First of all, 'born again' is a hype term. It's a media term that throws people into a corner and leaves them there. Whether people realize it or not, all these political and religious labels are irrelevant. . . ." He went on, however, to affirm the reality: "That was all part of my experience. It had to happen. When I get involved in something, I get totally involved. I don't just play around on the fringes."[12] Whatever his personal struggles, Christ had become real to Dylan, and he was not about to deny that.

With Christianity in his system, Dylan's art would necessarily reflect his faith. What were the consequences then of his conversion on his writing and his touring?

---

[11] "T-Bone Burnett's Rock 'n' Roll Testament," *L.A. Weekly*, March 26–April 1, 1982, p. 16 ff.
[12] Robert Hilburn, "Bob Dylan at 42—Rolling Down Highway 61 Again," *Los Angeles Times*, 30 Oct. 1983, Calendar, p. 3.

The response of the critics to Dylan's Christian music has been mixed, to say the least. On the one hand, Jann Wenner, reviewing *Slow Train Coming*, writes, "Bob Dylan has, at long last, come back into our lives and our times . . . with the most commercial LP he's ever released. . . . Bob Dylan once again has something urgent to sing. . . . *Slow Train Coming* . . . is the record that's been a long time coming, with an awesome, sudden stroke of transcendent and cohesive vision. This is what makes it so overwhelming . . . the lyrics again equal his early classics. . . . The more I hear the new album . . . the more I feel that it's one of the finest records Dylan has ever made. In time, it is possible that it might even be considered his greatest."[13] On the other hand, Paul Nelson, not even disguising his anger at Dylan, judges that there was only one passable cut on *Slow Train Coming* and *Saved*. For him they both beat "the same annoying drum." The portrait he sees emerging is one "filled mainly with hatred, confusion and egoism."[14]

Who is to be believed? Clearly, in his Slow Train period, Dylan divided the critics as he divided his fans. Much of the negative reaction was aimed at his "dogmatism" and came, in part, from a failure to understand the historic Christian faith and its necessary consequences.

With the arrival of *Infidels*, however, Dylan's reacceptance by the critics has been assured. Christopher Connelly writes in *Rolling Stone* that "*Infidels* is Bob Dylan's best album since the searing *Blood on the Tracks* nine years ago, a stunning recovery of the lyric and melodic powers that seemed to have all but deserted him."[15] Connelly attributes this to Dylan's leaving his Christian dogma behind, his own mood of deep sadness with which his listeners can universally identify, a crack backup band, and just plain passionate singing. In *Infidels*, as we shall see, Dylan's Christian thought is expressed parabolically and forms a substructure to many of his songs which is not always apparent on the surface. Thus, with this album, Dylan's confrontation with the critics seems over. As Dylan himself put it to Robert Hil-

---

[13] Wenner, "Bob Dylan and Our Times," p. 94.
[14] Paul Nelson, "Shot of Love, Bob Dylan," *Rolling Stone*, 15 Oct. 1981, p. 61.
[15] Christopher Connelly, "Dylan Makes Another Stunning Comeback," *Rolling Stone*, 24 Nov. 1983, p. 65.

burn, "I don't particularly regret telling people how to get their souls saved. I don't particularly regret any of that. Whoever was supposed to pick it up, picked it up. . . . But maybe the time for me to say that has just come and gone. Now it's time for me to do something else. . . . It's like sometimes those things appear very quickly and disappear. Jesus himself only preached for three years."[16]

After the original gospel tour, Dylan appeared in concert, restoring his older songs in a more mixed setting. Hilburn asked him if in future tours he would include any Slow Train songs. Dylan replied, "Yeah, I'll probably do a few of those. I get letters from people who say they were touched by those (gospel) shows. I don't disavow any of that. I've never made a record yet that I disavow."[17]

If the consequences of Dylan's conversion were confusing for the critics, the consequences of his touring were clear.

At first, Dylan was reticent to sing his new Christian songs. He knew full well that he would face hostility from his public. But both his identity as a Christian and the truth were at stake.

When Dylan went to his fans with his newfound faith he gave it authentic, historical expression in the context of black gospel music. Dylan instinctively knew what most Fundamentalists cannot admit—that black gospel music is essential to rock. The beat which to some is so suspect for its sexuality, is also the beat for dancing in the aisles of church and praising the Lord!

Thus, when Dylan began his first concerts as a Christian he opened them with a black trio and undergirded his gospel songs with a "Baptist" piano and organ, turning the whole evening into a service of praise.

Instinctively and on dead center, Dylan chose the black Christian genre, modified by rock music, through which to express his Christian experience. Dylan took his audience (one might even say *congregation*) behind rock 'n' roll to its gospel roots in a celebration of faith. At first, he excluded his pre-Christian music, because, as he said, he was uncertain of its validity. But he also excluded the earlier songs because they would

---

[16] Hilburn, "Bob Dylan at 42," p. 3.
[17] Ibid., p. 4.

not easily fit into the black gospel concert format he had created. Dylan made several comments from the stage on this tour, as we have seen. Later he no longer felt compelled to do this, but added, "When I walk around some of the towns we go to, however, I'm totally convinced people need Jesus. Look at those junkies and the winos and troubled people. It's all a sickness which can be healed in an instant."[18]

Beyond Dylan's personal life and his art lie his friends and fans. What were the consequences of his conversion for them? Looking back, it may be difficult to imagine the blow they experienced because of Dylan's new faith and the rejection he received in return.

First, his friends challenged him directly. Was his conversion real or only a new mask? Would he last as a Christian? As Dylan expresses it in "I Believe in You":

> They ask me how I feel
> And if my love is real
> And how I know I'll make it through?
> (on *Slow Train Coming*)

Since they can no longer identify with him, they don't want him around. He continues:

> They, they show me to the door
> They say, 'Don't come back no more'
> 'Cause I don't feel like they want me to.

Along with the personal hostility there are the intellectual objections. Dylan meets them in his militant "Pressin' On."

> Many try to stop me
> Shake me up in my mind
> Say, 'Prove to me that He's the Lord
> Show me a sign.'
> (on *Saved*)

Dylan responds to the challenge with two signs: his experience of Christ and Christ Himself. First, Dylan was lost; now he is found.

---

[18] Hilburn, "Dylan: 'I Learned That Jesus Is Real,' " p. 8.

Next, Christ has come and will come again. Dylan is certain of who *will* come because of who *has* come. He continues:

> What kind of sign they mean
> When it all comes from within
> When what's lost has been found
> What's to come has already been?

Ours is, in J. B. Phillips's phrase, a "visited planet."

As Dylan's friends reject him, he in turn sees them as trapped by the world and unwilling to pay the price of following Christ. He expresses this on the title song of *Slow Train Coming*.

> Sometimes I feel so lowdown and disgusted
> Can't help but wonder what's happenin' to my companions.
> Are they lost or are they found
> Have they counted the cost it'll take to bring down
> All their earthly principles
> They gonna have to abandon?

Not only did Dylan experience the rejection of his friends, a rabbi from Canada even came to try to talk him back into Judaism. This may be behind Dylan's writing

> Strangers they meddled in our affairs
> Poverty and shame was theirs
> But all I suffererd was not to be compared
> With the glory that is to be.
> ("In the Summertime" on *Shot of Love*)

While rejection was common, it only now emerges that Dylan had a positive impact upon at least some of his immediate circle. In April 1984 *Esquire Magazine* did an article on "Ramblin' Jack Elliott," the last of the Brooklyn cowboys. The subtitle read: "He's the son of Woody Guthrie and the father of Bob Dylan— the wandering folk hero with the whiskey voice."

In tracing Elliott's life the article details his influence upon Dylan. But Dylan, in return, decisively influenced Jewish-born Elliott, when Elliott, according to *Esquire*, "became a born-again Christian several years ago at the same Los Angeles church that ushered Dylan into the fold." With both alcohol and drugs undercutting him, Elliott reported, "When Bobby did it . . . I was far more weirdified by it than anything else. But I did it because I didn't want to die a neurotic wreck."[19]

Furthermore, beyond Dylan's close friends were his millions of fans. When he went public with his faith many experienced panic and anger. Why was this so?

First of all, as we have seen, Dylan had provided an identity for a whole generation. He uniquely verbalized the inarticulate feelings, questions, and fears of masses of people with an uncanny combination of simplicity, obscurity, and profundity. Moreover, this came in the doubly emotional package of poetry set to rock music. Such art changes moods, moving audiences from laughter to tears. It brings illumination, gives flight to the imagination, focuses vision, and probes into the heights and depths of human experience—all in a highly charged physical, communal setting.

Dylan's conversion meant betrayal, in Paul Williams's words, for those "whose method of appreciating Dylan over the years had been to identify 100% with most everything he says and feels."[20] Dylan the Christian represented for Williams and countless others an angry loss of identity. Williams admits, "And that's why we're so confused and upset about the gospel news he brought us this time. We keep thinking his news is our news, you see."[21] But in his direct Christian songs, Dylan's news is no longer "our news," it is Christ's news which is only "ours" by a similar experience of Christ. With his absolute truth in an age of relativism, Dylan immediately divides his audience as authentic Christianity has always done. (After all, Jesus wasn't crucified and the apostles martyred for preaching, "I'm OK. You're OK.")

At the same time, with his confession of Christ, Dylan steps out of the Messianic-pretender arena to which he had been assigned by so many. His recluse aloofness, his—in Gray's phrase—"scarcity value" as a superstar is gone.[22] In "When You Gonna Wake Up" we see Dylan has removed himself (or been removed) from the pedestal.

---

[19] Randy Sue Coburn, "On the Trail of Ramblin' Jack Elliott," *Esquire*, April 1984, p. 85.
[20] Paul Williams, *Dylan: What Happened?* (Glen Ellen, Calif.: Entwhistle Books, 1980), p. 15.
[21] Ibid., pp. 88-89.
[22] Gray, *The Art of Bob Dylan*, pp. 160-161.

> There's a man on a cross.
> He's been crucified for you
> Believe in His power
> That's about all you got to do.
> (on *Slow Train Coming*)

Dylan would say with Paul, "... not I, but Christ ..." (Galatians 2:20). The idol is gone and the idolatry is gone. Dylan is pointing away from himself to his Lord.

Furthermore, Dylan appears to abandon the culture he helped to create. The angry protest, the apocalyptic horror, and their chaotic consequences are severely modified. The answer is no longer found in unformed mysticism or in a lover's arms. Now Dylan's cutting edge of protest is even more profound, but it points away from the luxury of self-pity, cynicism, quiet despair, or half-answers to Christ and His Kingdom. This also means a moral revolution. The gospel strikes at the heart of hedonism and narcissism fed by rock music in the "nightclubs of the brokenhearted and the stadiums of the damned" ("Trouble" on *Shot of Love*).

The final consequence of Dylan's conversion for many was "theological." In calling for surrender to Christ, he was calling his listeners to give up the illusion of their own autonomy, to humble themselves before God and embrace the one way marked out for them by Him. In "When He Returns" Dylan writes:

> Truth is an arrow
> And that gate is narrow
> That it passes through.
> (on *Slow Train Coming*)

Again:

> There's only one road
> And it leads to Calvary.
> ("Saving Grace" on *Saved*)

During his first tour after his conversion, Dylan lost many fans by refusing to play his old songs, as noted above. A year later he told Robert Hilburn that he wasn't in touch with them then, but he had changed. As Dylan recalled, "This show evolved out of that last tour. It's like the songs aren't . . . how can I put it? Those songs weren't anti-God at all. I wasn't sure about that for a while . . . I love those songs. They're still part of me."[23]

Thus, Dylan was able to see the value of his pre-Slow Train songs and the function that they played in his life, like John the Baptist, pointing to Christ. Dylan expressed this overall purpose for his art in a London interview for WNEW in July 1981: "I think that art can lead you to God. . . . If it's not doing that it's leading you the other way. It's not certainly leading you nowhere. It's bringing you somewhere. It's either bringing you that-a-way or this-a-way. . . . If it's expressing truth it's leading you to God. . . ."

Aleksandr Solzhenitsyn voiced a similar viewpoint in his Nobel lecture on literature, *East and West:* "One artist imagines himself the creator of an autonomous spiritual world. . . . But he collapses under the load. . . . Another artist recognizes above himself a higher power and joyfully works as a humble apprentice under God's heaven. . . ." Thus, he concludes. "Art can warm even a chilled and sunless soul to an exalted spiritual experience. . . . You glimpse for a moment the Inaccessible, a realm forever beyond reach. And your soul begins to ache. . . ."

Through the experience of Dylan's art, the soul aches. It aches with musical mood shifts from blues sadness to rock-out exhilaration. It aches with the transcendent power of poetry expressing a sacramental creation and an ambivalent human heart. It aches with moral indignation, apocalyptic despair, visionary longing, and then, finally, resolution from above: "Shine your light, shine your light on me" ("Precious Angel" on *Slow Train Coming*). Dylan's odyssey brought him to God, and all of his music taken together can serve the same purpose for others.

At one time Dylan denied that he provided answers for people. He told Anthony Scaduto in 1971, ". . . people shouldn't look to me for answers. . . . I'm sorry they think I can give them any answers. Because I can't. I got enough to keep busy without looking for other people's problems."[24] However, the times and Dylan have changed. In his London radio interview in 1981, Dylan claimed to have the answers to the larger questions of life.

---

[23] Hilburn, "Dylan: 'I Learned That Jesus Is Real,' " p. 8.
[24] Scaduto, *Bob Dylan*, p. 309.

He said, "... the answers to those questions ... they've got to be in the songs I've written ... someplace.... If you know ... where to look. I think you'll find the answers to those questions is right there in the songs."

Dylan's detractors may charge him with being a narrow-minded, dogmatic Fundamentalist, but neither his life, nor his lyrics will support the charge. In fact, Dylan has an acute perception of classic, biblical Christianity. Michael Gray, unsympathetic with his conversion, admits that in "... opting for this refuge [Dylan] has not signalled any abrogation of his intellect.... There is a lot of intellectual and emotional honesty in these [Christian] albums."[25] We turn now to investigate that intellectual honesty in order to understand the structure of Dylan's Christian world view and the substance of his thought.

---

[25] Gray, *The Art of Bob Dylan*, p. 225.

Chapter 4—Vision

"Shake the dust off your feet
Don't look back. . . ."

Dylan performs his award-winning "You Gotta Serve Somebody" at the 22nd annual Grammy Awards show.

A COMPREHENSIVE AND COHERENT vision dominates Bob Dylan's recent albums. They are controlled by his Christian world view which makes sense of history and human experience in light of Christ. While each song presents an aspect of the truth, taken together there is a profundity and a wholeness that reveals the depth and conviction of Dylan's mind now infused with his biblical faith. Here we will investigate several central theses of that faith which determine the three LP releases of his Slow Train period. In the next chapter we will focus on the continuity between this period and Dylan's next phase as it is expressed in *Infidels*.

There is a certain progression from *Slow Train Coming* (1979) to *Saved* (1980) to *Shot of Love* (1981). In *Slow Train Coming* Dylan commands his poetic genius and reasserts his cultural critique as he relates his own experience of Christ. His use of symbolism, however, allows for a degree of ambiguity that opens minds to his message while guarding against a premature turnoff. For example, for Dylan the "Slow Train Coming" is Christ. But the symbol of the train allowed Jann Wenner in his *Rolling Stone* review to see it "as thoroughly American. The 'train' is not just a suggestion, but it's an affirmation of America's greatness."[1] While Wenner has missed the point, which is made clear by the final song on the album, "When He Returns," he is drawn into the discussion and even forced to face his own faith. As he admits, "I am not so full of certainty about these times, our social standards or the conduct of my companions that I can dismiss

---

[1] Jann Wenner, "Bob Dylan and Our Times: The Slow Train Is Coming," *Rolling Stone*, 20 Sept. 1979, p. 95.

the validity of Dylan's religiously phrased ideas." While Wenner doubts that he will attend church or kneel by his bed, he also agrees that the old solutions have failed. He concludes that as "we look back at long years of disrepair, then maybe the time for religion has come again, and rather too suddenly—'like a thief in the night.' " *Slow Train Coming* forces the issue of faith. It builds the bridge to *Saved*.

In *Saved* Dylan pulls out all the stops. Here he takes the listener into the heart of his faith with his strong black gospel–rock beat. The album cover itself, with Christ's bloody hand reaching down from heaven to the grasping hands reaching up from earth, reveals what is to come. Several songs are dominated by biblical phrasing and language. The Slow Train in the first album becomes the sacrificial Lamb in the second, as Dylan sings, "I've been saved by the blood of the Lamb" ("Saved"). The final song, "Are You Ready," is an evangelistic call. Dylan warns:

> Are you ready to meet Jesus?
> Are you where you want to be?
> Will He know you when He sees you
> Or will He say, 'Depart from me'?

Lest there be any ambiguity as to the issue or the future, Dylan continues:

> When destruction comes swiftly
> And there's no time to say, 'Fare-thee-well'
> Have you decided whether you wanna be
> In heaven or in hell?

"Saved" is Dylan's heart-statement of the gospel. It is simple, direct, cutting at times, with warmth, personal vulnerability, and confrontation all wrapped into one.

If *Slow Train Coming* is expansive and symbolic, *Saved* is concentrated and biblical. With *Shot of Love*, we have Dylan's symbolic power wedded to a wider mix of musical styles and a broader scope. There is even one song, "Lenny Bruce," which could have appeared on any of Dylan's pre-Christian albums, picking up on his often repeated outlaw theme. The other songs, however, are fully controlled by his Christian faith, and the album's second side contains the interfacing of songs of warning, "Dead Man, Dead Man" and "Trouble," with exquisite expressions of Dylan's conversion, "In the Summertime" and "Every Grain of Sand." Here, in a more subtle way than on *Saved*, Dylan calls his hearers to Christ through his own personal witness. Thus, we see in *Shot of Love* a seasoned reflection that demonstrates the maturity of his faith. The sum total of all three albums presents Dylan as a thoroughly converted man. We turn then to his Christian world view which determines his current music.

The Cosmic Conflict

Dylan's first Christian album, *Slow Train Coming*, opens with "Gotta Serve Somebody." It was this song that he also chose to sing to the nation in 1980 on the night of the Grammy Awards. As the *Los Angeles Times* reported on February 8, 1980, "The most dramatic moment in the nationally televised program . . . came when Bob Dylan received a standing ovation when he walked on stage . . . to sing 'Gotta Serve Somebody.' " After going on to win the award as the best male rock singer for that year Dylan responded, "I didn't expect this and I want to thank the Lord." Why did Dylan's first Christian album begin with this song, and why did he choose to sing it at the Grammy Awards? The answer lies in its sweeping description of the whole of humanity, from the rich to the poor, from the famous to the forgotten, and the choice each person must make.

> It may be the Devil
> And it may be the Lord
> But you gotta serve somebody.

For Dylan all of history and human experience is fundamentally understood by the warfare between God and Satan. The great issues of the human condition, the political order, and historical destiny cannot be grasped apart from dealing with the devil. Dylan's passion for the truth, his obsession to get to the root of all things, and his own spiritual honesty unite around this seminal theme. To use Dylan's own imagery, if he is to show us what is really going on, he must unmask the devil, who, in the

Apostle Paul's phrase, disguises himself as an angel of light (2 Corinthians 11:14).

To deal with the devil, however, we must begin with the wider context which Dylan gives in the song "Trouble" on *Shot of Love*. There he paints a broad canvas of evil and our absurd precautions against it.

> Trouble in the city
> Trouble on the farm
> You've got your rabbit's foot
> You've got your good-luck charm
> But they can't help you none
> When there's trouble.

The song continues with a catalog of catastrophy: polluted water and air, revolution, drought, starvation, "packaging of the soul," persecution, execution, "governments out of control." Why all this evil?

> Put your ear to the train tracks
> Put your ear to the ground
> You ever feel like you're never alone
> Even when there's nobody else around?
> It's the beginning of the universe
> That's been cursed by trouble.

This universe bears a curse, and if we begin to listen closely we will sense the presence of malevolent evil. Behind our personal sin, therefore, stands the archetypal sin: Satan, created as a good angel to do God's will, exercising his gift of freedom by rebelling against heaven and leading a host of other spiritual beings in his declaration of civil war. Thus, in Genesis, the serpent in the garden of Eden whispers to Eve before she whispers to herself and falls into sin. For the Bible the totality of human evil cannot be explained apart from personal, supernatural evil.

Now we can see how illuminating this was for Dylan. His early abandonment of politics was based on the recognition that the whole system is corrupt. As we have already noted from "George Jackson," Dylan said in 1971:

Sometimes I think this whole world
Is one big prison-yard
Some of us are prisoners
The rest of us are guards.

As a Christian, Dylan came to see that the prison yard is the domain of the devil. It is Satan who, in the gospels, offers to Jesus the kingdoms of this world. The absurdity of life that Dylan has seen, the "Desolation Row" where we live and the enormity of evil, the "idiot wind" blowing through history and our hearts is finally clear. It is Satan, not God, who is the author of chaos. It is Satan who lures us into the abyss.

Thus, Dylan's rejection of politics lies in his recognition that politics are "the politics of sin" ("Dead Man, Dead Man" on *Shot of Love*). As he puts it in *Slow Train Coming* on the title song: "Fools glorify themselves tryin' to manipulate Satan."

In his London radio interview, Dylan was asked about specific political issues. His answer to the abortion question was that issues such as these are just diversions from the real issues. He said, ". . . if they can get you thinking about those things then they put you away with the bigger things which you're not thinking about. . . . You cast the spotlight on something and make everybody look that way and then you come at them from another direction." When challenged that this sounded conspiratorial, Dylan replied, "Yah, it does, don't it."

C. S. Lewis makes a similar point in *Screwtape Letters*. Screwtape, a professional devil, advises his nephew Wormwood, a junior tempter, never to allow his "patient" (a potential Christian) to think about universal issues and withdraw "his attention from the stream of immediate sense experiences." He goes on, "Your business is to fix his attention on the stream. Teach him to call it 'real life' and don't let him ask what he means by 'real'."

This universal curse, however, is also intensely personal for Dylan. So he begins his song "Saved":

I was blinded by the Devil
Born already ruined
Stone-cold-dead
As I stepped out of the womb.

(on *Saved*)

81

Such spiritual darkness is predicated upon Satan's revolt; we are born "already ruined."

In our natural state (or "unnatural," as the case may be), we are not really conscious of the devil and his power over us. So Dylan writes, "The Devil's shinin' light/It can be most blinding" ("Saving Grace" on *Saved*). If we are blind, Satan won't bother us. Why should he? As Dylan puts it in "Dead Man, Dead Man":

> Dead Man, Dead Man
> When will you arise?
> Cobwebs in your mind
> Dust upon your eyes.

> Satan doesn't bother you
> There's a bird's nest in your hair. . . .
> <div align="right">(on <i>Shot of Love</i>)</div>

Thus, we were all unconsciously subservient to a superior power.

Knowing the origin of evil, however, does not lead Dylan into a pious withdrawal from the world. To the contrary, he now uses his root insight and the power of his poetry to expose evil for what it is. Thus, after his conversion, Dylan returned with full force to the social criticism that had marked his work in the sixties. This led people to assert, "Dylan is back." The one difference, however, was that now Dylan knew the ultimate source of evil and the ultimate solution to evil. His criticism is no longer the criticism of angry despair. It has a new depth to it.

In the New Testament in John's Gospel, Jesus calls Satan a liar and a murderer from the beginning (John 8:44). His goal is our eternal death. The means he employs are designed to deceive us about the world and ourselves. So Dylan writes in "Precious Angel":

> The enemy is subtle
> How-be-it we're deceived
> When the truth's in our hearts
> And we still don't believe

and continues:

My so-called friends
Have fallen under a spell
They look me squarely in the eyes
And say, 'Well, all is well.'
(on *Slow Train Coming*)

But Dylan must show us that all is *not* well. A necessary step to truth is to have the spell broken, the deception exposed. This Dylan does with deadly accuracy. What, then, does he show us?

To begin with, Dylan insists that we are all being seduced. Religion itself now serves this end (*religion* being defined as our attempt to reach God rather than God's reaching us). This makes traditional religion the antithesis of true Christianity, or in Marx's dictum, the opiate of the people. The Swiss theologian Karl Barth would agree—religion is our last defense against the living God.

To be specific, Dylan sees the pulpit as morally bankrupt. On *Slow Train Coming* he describes preachers who preach "spiritual pride" ("Gotta Serve Somebody"). Furthermore, congregations share the moral bankruptcy with "adulterers in churches" ("When You Gonna Wake Up"). Because of the impotence of institutional Christianity, our spiritual hunger is now fed from the East by "Spiritual advisors and gurus/To guide your every move." Their guidance, however, is bondage. They offer "Instant inner peace/And every step you take has got to be approved" ("When You Gonna Wake Up"). After analyzing many ills, Dylan concludes:

But the enemy I see
Wears a cloak of decency
All non-believers and men-stealers
Talkin' in the name of religion.
("Slow Train")

In despair, many turn from heaven to earth—from God's kingdom to man's kingdom. Politics, however, is no better than religion. Its order is breaking down. In "Trouble" Dylan warns of

Drought and starvation
Packaging of the soul

> Persecution, execution
> Governments out of control
> You can see the writing
> On the wall inviting
> Trouble. . . .
>
> (on *Shot of Love*)

Furthermore, the competing ideologies of East and West both seduce us because of their absolutist claims and false hopes.

> Counterfeit philosophies have polluted all of your thoughts
> Karl Marx has got you by the throat
> And Henry Kissinger's got you tied up into knots.
> ("When You Gonna Wake Up" on *Slow Train Coming*)

Again, in "Slow Train" Dylan warns of political subterfuge:

> Big-time negotiators
> False healers and woman haters
> Masters of the bluff
> And masters of the proposition.

No wonder Dylan pleads:

> Doctor can you hear me
> I need some Medicaid
> I see the kingdoms of the world
> And it's makin' me feel afraid.
> ("Shot of Love")

Thus, to look for answers in the political order is to try to "manipulate Satan," since it is here that he exercises his domain ("Slow Train"). It is to engage in the "politics of sin" where today's liberation is tomorrow's bondage ("Dead Man, Dead Man" on *Shot of Love*).

With such satanic seduction, we also see the collapse of the moral order around us. We can no longer count on justice.

> Man's ego's inflated
> His laws are outdated
> They don't apply no more. . . .
> ("Slow Train")

The result? "You got innocent men in jail/Your insane asylums are filled." Thus, the legal structure is now relativized. Dylan continues, "You got gangsters in power/And lawbreakers makin' the rules" ("When You Gonna Wake Up" on *Slow Train Coming*).

The final consequence of religious and political seduction is dehumanization. Dylan warns of the "packaging of the soul" ("Trouble" on *Shot of Love*). He gets to the heart of the issue in "Slow Train":

> I don't care about economy
> I don't care about astronomy
> But it sure does bother me
> To see my loved ones turning into puppets.

Now, as we will discuss in detail below, we, too, play into this evil game. The seduced become the seducers. As Dylan laments in "When You Gonna Wake Up," "The rich seduce the poor/And the old are seduced by the young" (on *Slow Train Coming*). The family too, is collapsing under similar pressures.

> So much depression
> Can't keep track of it no more
> Sons becoming husbands to their mothers
> Old men turnin' young daughters into whores.
> ("Gonna Change My Way of Thinkin' " on *Slow Train Coming*)

Satan, however, can deceive us because we want to be deceived. We think we're free when we're not. Dylan continues:

> Well, don't know which is worse
> Doin' your own thing, or just being cool
> You remember all about the brass ring
> You forget all about the Golden Rule.

Selfishness and self-gratification now become our goals in a pop-Freudian culture.

> They say, 'Loose your inhibition
> Follow your own ambition'
> They talk about a life of brotherly love
> Show me someone who knows how to live it.
> ("Slow Train")

In despair or relief, many assume that the grave is the end. This, however, is only a sign of their spiritual captivity. As Dylan writes in "Property of Jesus":

> Oh, you can laugh at salvation
> You can play your Olympic Games
> You can think that when you rest at last
> You'll go back from where you came.
>
> But you've picked up quite a story
> And you've changed since the womb
> What happened to the real you?
> You've been captured, but by whom?
> (on *Shot of Love*)

There are, finally, only two alternatives. Dylan confronts us with them in "Precious Angel."

> Now there's a spiritual warfare
> Flesh and blood breakin' down
> You either got faith or you got unbelief
> And there ain't no neutral ground.
> (on *Slow Train Coming*)

Indeed, you "gotta serve somebody."

Certainly Dylan knows how offensive this thesis is. For many reasons, few people today believe in a personal devil. Dylan's views fly in the face of progress, evolution, human autonomy, the supremacy of reason, and all secular utopias. We should remember, however, that the church has always held that the devil's best ploy is for people to deny his existence.

Camus understands this better than most Christians. In his novel *The Plague*, without warning, the rats—representing monstrous, irrational evil—come out of the cellars and infect the populace. Camus notes that the townspeople were humanists. He writes, "They disbelieved in pestilences. A pestilence isn't a thing made to man's measure; therefore we tell ourselves that pestilence is a mere bogy of the mind, a bad dream that will pass away. But it doesn't always pass away and from one bad dream to another, it is men who pass away, and the humanists first of all, because they haven't taken their precautions." Camus observes that the people "forgot to be modest." They thought "that everything was still possible for them." He continues, "They fancied themselves free, and no one will ever be free so long as there are pestilences."

Malcolm Muggeridge, former editor of the British humor magazine *Punch*, ironically admits that he has found it easier to believe in the devil than in God, as he says in his book *Jesus, the Man Who Lives*, ". . . for one thing, alas, I have had more to do with him." Muggeridge continues, "It seems to me quite extraordinary that anyone should have failed to notice, especially during the last half century, a diabolic presence in the world, pulling downwards as gravity does. . . . A counter-force to creativity; destructive in its nature and purpose, raging far and wide like a forest fire, and burning in the heart's core—pinpointed there, a fiery tongue of fierce desire." Muggeridge holds that we have seen the devil's destructiveness consuming past, present, and future. He concludes, "Have we not smelt him, rancid-sweet? Touched him, slippery-soft? Measured with the eye his fearful shape? Heard his fearful rhetoric? Glimpsed him, sometimes in a mirror, with drooling, greedy mouth, misty ravening eyes and flushed flesh? Who can miss him in those blackest of all moments, when God seems to have disappeared, leaving the Devil to occupy an empty universe?"

Dylan's belief in Satan then is no "fundamentalist cop-out." It is his necessary conclusion formed from his own sense of profound, tyrannical evil and illumined by biblical revelation. History is not merely the sum total of human acts. It is the stage upon which a cosmic conflict is being fought, and we will never understand ourselves or history apart from the ultimate dimensions of that battle:

> It may be the Devil
> And it may be the Lord
> But you gotta serve somebody.

The Human Heart

Most people believe that the human heart is either basically good or simply a tabula rasa upon which society writes its script.

Change is possible, then, either by appeal to a person's free volition, or moral conscience, or by the manipulation of the social environment. When a generation of "freedom riders" went South singing "Blowin' in the Wind," they were committed to social change. That their high idealism, moral outrage, and teach-ins would fail to integrate society and stop the Vietnam carnage was unthinkable.

Dylan, however, became quickly disillusioned with the protest movement, not only because of his sense of corporate and universal evil, but also because of his analysis of the human heart. As he turned inward, haunted by the vision of what love should be and cynical over love's demands, he had to conclude, "It ain't me, Babe/It ain't me you're lookin' for, Babe" ("It Ain't Me" on *Another Side of Bob Dylan*). With song after song in his pre-Christian era, Dylan exposed the duplicity, hypocrisy, ambivalence, and self-seeking of the human heart.

Later, during his London radio interview, Dylan commented on the relationship between beauty and our hearts. Asked if beauty can lead a person to God, he replied, "Beauty can be very, very deceiving. It is not always of God. . . . Beauty appeals to our eyes. . . ." The interviewer interjected, "And to our hearts?" Dylan responded, "Our heart's not good. If your heart's not good what good does beauty do that comes through your eyes going down to your heart which isn't good anyway?" The next step, then, in Dylan's analysis is the corruption of human nature, the fallen state of the human heart.

Dylan can boldly assert that the heart is made of stone. In "Property of Jesus" he acidly mocks those who reject Christians:

> He's the property of Jesus
> Resent him to the bone
> You've got somethin' better
> You've got a heart of stone.
>
> (on *Shot of Love*)

Again, he speaks of himself on the title song of *Saved* as "Stone cold dead/As I stepped out of the womb."

What does it mean to have a heart of stone? At its core, it is simply to have one's heart cut off from the living God. It is to be filled with pride, seduced by Satan, and destined to death, standing under divine judgment. Dylan describes this in a compact verse:

> Soon as a man is born
> You know the sparks begin to fly
> He gets wise in his own eyes
> And he's made to believe a lie
> Who would deliver him
> From the death he's bound to die?
> ("What Can I Do For You" on *Saved*)

In other words, to have a heart of stone is to deny God as the ground and meaning of our being, "The Reality of Man." This, of course, leads to self-deception and its bitter fruit—self-hatred. Dylan asks:

> How long can you falsify
> And deny what is real?
> How long can you hate yourself
> For the weakness you conceal?
> ("When He Returns" on *Slow Train Coming*)

A specific example of the corruption of our hearts is offered in "Heart of Mine." To the heart that longs for an adulterous relationship, Dylan writes, "Don't untie the ties that bind/Heart of mine," and warns

> Heart of mine, be still
> You can play with fire
> But you'll get the bill.
> (on *Shot of Love*)

This specific struggle, however, reveals a more general condition. Dylan continues:

> Heart of mine
> So malicious and so full of guile
> Give you an inch
> And you'll take a mile.

The road to recovery begins by accepting this stern diagnosis and eliminating shallow solutions.

> Don't show me no picture show
> Nor give me no books to read
> They don't satisfy the hurt inside
> Nor the habit that I feed.
> ("Shot of Love")

Abandoning all human possibilities, Dylan turns to Christ, "Whatever pleases you/Tell it to my heart" ("What Can I Do For You" on *Saved*). Again he admits:

> I've been broken
> Shattered like an empty cup
> I'm just waitin' on the Lord
> To rebuild and fill me up.
> ("Covenant Woman" on *Saved*)

In conclusion, we are faced with a double bondage. Satan has led the cosmos in revolt. The kingdoms of this world are temporarily his domain. We have been deceived by him and are held in his power. At the same time, our heart is evil. We say yes to Satan's arrogance and declare our own independence from God. Reason now is used as rationalization in order to cover up our rebellion. As Pascal says, "The heart has reasons that reason cannot know." Thus, we have a heart of stone. This, then, is the context in which Dylan presents the meaning of Christ. It is Jesus who has broken both the power of Satan and the hardness of the human heart.

The Love of Christ

As we have already seen, love is the central issue and the deepest experience for Dylan. Human love, however, is fickle and selfish. Jonathan Cott, in his *Rolling Stone* interview, observed, "It seems as if the tyranny of love makes people unhappy." Dylan responded, "That's the tyranny of man–woman love. That ain't too much love." Earlier in the interview, Dylan told Cott, "Love comes from the Lord—it keeps all of us going. If you want it, you got it."[2] It is this love that brought Dylan to Christ.

---

[2] Jonathan Cott, "Bob Dylan, 1978," in *The Rolling Stone Interviews*, p. 363.

For Dylan, the center of the Christian faith is to be found in Jesus Christ Himself. In the midst of Satan's seduction, in the midst of all the illusion and manipulation of the world, in the midst of our self-seeking, here, in our history, the truth has come and that truth is a Person. In "Every Grain of Sand" on *Shot of Love*, Dylan declares Christ to be "The Reality of Man." He is our Reality for two reasons. As God, He is the absolute, the Creator before whom we stand and to whom we are accountable. But, also, as a man, Christ shows us our true humanity. He is the sinless Son of God who reveals what God has designed us to be and to become.

Thus, the light of Christ shines in our darkness. Dylan prays in "Precious Angel," "Shine your light, shine your light on me." His request is answered when he is told of a Man who came "and died a criminal's death" (on *Slow Train Coming*). It is Jesus who breaks through our "heart of stone." For this reason, the gospel story must be told. It is the very Word of God to us and, as Karl Barth says, the Word of God creates its own audience.

Dylan narrates the gospel in "In the Garden" on *Saved*, thrusting the truth home in a series of rhetorical questions: Did they know? Did they hear? Did they see? Did they dare? Did they believe?

Dylan asks, first of all, if the world knew that Jesus was God's Son and its Lord? The answer, of course, is implied in the question.

> When they came for Him in the garden
> Did they know?
> Did they know He was the Son of God?
> Did they know that He was Lord?
> Did they hear when He told Peter
> 'Peter, put up your sword'?

Next, Dylan asks if they heard Jesus in the city when He told Nicodemus that he had to be born again. Of course, they didn't. Then he asks, "When He healed the blind and crippled, did they see?" And, to be sure, the answer is no. Next, establishing the offense of Jesus' claims, Dylan goes on to speak of Jesus' oneness with the Father.

> When He said, 'Pick up your bed and walk'
> Why must you criticize?
> Same thing my Father do
> I can do likewise!

Then, the shadow of rejection looms when Dylan passionately asks, "Did they speak out against Him/Did they dare?" But the final verse is triumphant.

> When He rose from the dead
> Did they believe?
> When He rose from the dead
> Did they believe?

> He said, 'All power is given to me
> In heaven and on earth'
> Did they know right then and there
> Just what their power was worth?

In His Resurrection Jesus has shown the true power to be His power over death. Here is the resolution of our deepest fear. Now the exalted Lord holds all power and human "power" is seen to be vanity.

Therefore, in the gospel story, Jesus is revealed as the Son of God and the risen Lord who has come to do His Father's will. His saving power is manifested both in physical miracles and in the spiritual miracle of the new birth.

The central reality of the gospel, however, is Christ's love for a lost world. For Dylan, as for the New Testament, this is most clearly seen in the cross. He writes of Christ's love given to pay the price of sin in the title song on *Saved*.

> By His power I've been lifted
> In His love I am secure
> For He bought me with a price
> Freed me from the pit.

And it is Christ, the Old Testament sacrificial Lamb, giving His life as an atonement for sin, who is sung of in the chorus, "I've been saved/By the blood of the Lamb."

This, however, is no abstract doctrinal point. Dylan ex-

February 1980. Bob Dylan accepts his Grammy for Best Male Rock Vocal Performance for "You Gotta Serve Somebody."

presses his own personal involvement in Christ's death when he writes

> For me He was chastised
> For me He was hated
> For me He was rejected
> By a world that He created.
> ("Solid Rock" on *Saved*)

Similarly, Paul tells the Galatians that he lives by faith in the Son of God ". . . who loved me, and gave himself for me" (Galatians 2:20). Thus, for those who come to Christ there is acceptance rather than rejection. He does not return like for like. They must, however, come to His cross, the focal point both of their humiliation and of God's forgiveness. Dylan writes:

> The wicked know no peace
> And you just can't fake it
> There's only one road
> And it leads to Calvary.
> ("Saving Grace" on *Saved*)

Take this road and believe! That's all that is called for. As Dylan states it:

> There's a man on a cross
> And He's been crucified for you.
> Believe in His power
> That's about all you got to do.
> ("When You Gonna Wake Up" on *Slow Train Coming*)

Salvation then, is Christ's work not ours. He exposes the seduction of Satan. He reveals our true bondage. He dies to deliver us from the divine penalty for sin.

But Christ not only died for us two thousand years ago, He also intervenes in our lives now. Dylan recalls:

> Nobody to rescue me
> Nobody would dare
> I'm going down for the last time
> But by His mercy I've been spared.

Vision

> Not by works
> By faith in Him alone
> For so long I've been hindered
> For so long I've been stoned.
> ("Saved")

Dylan puts this in more traditional language in another verse of the same song:

> By His grace I have been touched
> By His Word I have been healed
> By His hand I've been delivered
> By His Spirit I've been sealed.

In light of Christ's work then, what is to be our response? Dylan asks this in the song, "What Can I Do For You?" His answer? "You've done it all and there's nothing more to do" (on *Saved*). All that he can really do is to be grateful. So he sings: "And I'm so glad—thank you Lord. I just wanna thank you, Lord" ("Saved").

The illusion of human love, therefore, is now replaced by the reality of divine love.

> The Devil's shining light
> It can be most blinding
> To search for love
> It ain't no more than vanity.
>
> As I look around this world
> All that I'm seein'
> Is the Saving Grace
> That's over me.
> ("Saving Grace" on *Saved*)

In Dylan's conversion, as we have seen, this "saving grace" is Jesus Christ confronting him and calling him. Into Dylan's empty heart, Christ pumps His life-giving blood.

> I've got the heart
> You've got the blood

95

We cut through iron
And we cut through mud.
("In the Summertime" on *Shot of Love*)

It is Christ who resolves the problems of Satan's deception and our heart of stone. It is Christ who is Dylan's "Shot of Love." What then are we to make of this?

If it is difficult for the modern mind to accept the reality of Satan and the sinfulness of the human heart, it is almost impossible for it to entertain Christ's death as the necessary sacrifice for human sin. Why is this so?

In the first place, any sense of God's awesome holiness and justice has been drained from our consciousness. That all the world will stand before the Divine Judgment Seat seems medieval. The absolute demand of God's moral law seems archaic and arbitrary in a society shot through with relativism. It is only with the recovery of the sense of God's just order for our lives that we can begin to fathom our moral responsibility before Him. And only when this is reestablished can we understand our accountability to that order and the disastrous consequences of our failure.

Before his conversion, C. S. Lewis objected to the existence of God because of all the terrible evil in the world. He then came to see that such an objection had to be based upon a transcendent moral order beyond this world. How could Lewis absolutely object to suffering children, terminal cancer, and natural disasters if he were merely swimming in the soup of moral relativism? An absolute objection demanded an absolute standard, and that standard had to exist outside of human relativity. Thus, as Lewis came to accept such a transcendent standard as the ground of his moral indignation, he was one step closer to believing in the God of the Bible.

It is probable that Dylan also made a similar journey. His own moral outrage, his own sense of injustice, his own unmasking of human pretense presupposed a standard beyond "the morals of despair."

When this standard is accepted and the deceived and deceiving human heart is measured by it, a sense of sin and guilt must be the result. Not only did Dylan unmask the moral corruption of the culture, as we have seen, he also unmasked the human heart. No Freudian analysis of our twisted motives and selfish preoccupation could be more damning than what Dylan found.

If we cannot fulfill the divine design for human life then there must be consequences to our moral failure or else that design collapses and contributes to "the morals of despair." As a rule, however, we expect more justice from the sheriff than we do from God. But what we expect because of our naive humanism (and devious rationalization) and what we will actually get are two different things. Here then we are prepared for the second major truth of Christianity: Not only is God a God of awesome holiness and justice, He is also a God of boundless mercy and love.

In his tract "On Liberty," Martin Luther posed the classic question, How can God be holy and receive sinners at the same time? In His holiness He must condemn the sinner. In His love, however, He desires to forgive and save the sinner. For Luther, and for all historic Christianity, the answer to this dilemma lies in "Christ crucified." As Luther puts it, "Holiness and love kiss in the cross." Having lived out the just demand of God's law in His sinless life, Christ died on the cross, not for His sins (for He had none), but for ours. Luther holds that when we come to the cross by faith we are married, or united, to Christ. As in marriage union, then, we receive all that Christ has and He receives all that we have. We receive all of His holiness and He receives all of our sins.

The modern mind has difficulty seeing God's love in Christ's cross because the sense of divine judgment has been lost and love has been reduced to mere sentimentality. When we come to understand the costliness of God's forgiveness, however, the cross will regain its meaning. God doesn't pass off sin as a misdemeanor. It is a capital crime. Thus, He comes in Christ to bear sin away and to pay its penalty in His own death. As James Denney puts it, "The Cross [is] inscribed 'God is love,' only because it is inscribed also, 'The wages of sin is death.'" He continues, "The love which is [its] motive . . . [bears] immediately upon the sinful; gratitude exerts an irresistible constraint; His responsibility means our emancipation; His death our life; His bleeding wound our healing. Whoever says 'He bore

our sins' says substitution; and to say substitution is to say something which involves an immeasurable obligation to Christ, and
has therefore in it an incalculable motive power."[3]

That this is so for Dylan needs no proof. His albums, his
tours, and his interviews after his conversion all demonstrate this
power. Again, as Bill Graham, the producer of Dylan's first
Christian tour put it, "It is awesome. I am a Jew, and I am deeply
moved by what this man is doing. It's a very profound display of
personal convictions." Dylan put his hand to the plow. He didn't
look back. He knew that life must be lived as a Christian.

The Christian Life

For Dylan the Christian life is a life of grace. It is Christ who
has renewed him. It is Christ who has filled up the hunger he had
denied. It is Christ who has given all there is to give. Dylan responds:

> Well, you've done it all
> And there's no more anyone can pretend to do.
> What can I do for you?
> ("What Can I Do For You" on *Saved*)

On one level then there is nothing that Dylan can do. If Paul
is the theologian of grace, Dylan is the poet of grace. The answer
to the question "What can I do for you?" Nothing!

This is the passive side of the Christian life. It is a life lived
by faith alone. As Paul put it, ". . . the just shall live by faith"
(Romans 1:17). Dylan expresses this in "I Believe in You." Although rejected by his friends he perseveres because he believes.

> And I, I walk out on my own
> A thousand miles from home
> But I don't feel alone
> 'Cause I believe in you.
> (on *Slow Train Coming*)

---

[3] Cited in John R. Taylor, *God Loves Like That!* (Richmond, Va.: John Knox Press, 1962),
pp. 62, 54.

Through tears and laughter, although God seems distant at times, and even though Dylan fails his Lord, he continues on with assurance.

> Oh, when the dawn is nearing
> Oh, when the night is disappearing
> Oh, this feelin's still here in my heart.

Since what he has received is priceless, no one can deflect him.

> And—what you have given me today
> Is worth more than I can pay
> And no matter what they say
> I believe in you.

As Dylan gratefully expresses the life of faith in "Saving Grace":

> My faith keeps me alive
> But I still be weepin'
> For the saving grace
> That's over me.
>
> (on *Saved*)

Here then, for Dylan, the Christian life is "passive" at its heart. It is living by faith in complete dependence upon God. It is knowing that He is all-in-all.

At the same time, paradoxically, the Christian life is active. The grace of Christ does not lead to apathy, but to action. Thus, Dylan writes:

> I know all about poison
> I know all about fiery darts
> I don't care how rough the road is
> Show me where it starts.

As he moves, however, he moves in gratitude:

> Whatever pleases you
> Tell it to my heart
> Well, I don't deserve it
> But I sure did make it through.
> ("What Can I Do For You" on *Saved*)

This active Christian life reflects Paul's witness, "I press on toward the goal for the prize of the upward call of God in Christ Jesus" (Philippians 3:14 NAS). Thus, Dylan writes that he's "pressin' on . . . to the higher calling of my Lord" ("Pressin' On," on *Saved*). The triumph of his calling is certain.

> Shake the dust off your feet.
> Don't look back
> Nothing can hold you down
> Nothing that you lack.

Although he is confident of the future, still there is a battle in the present. Dylan continues:

> Temptation's not an easy thing
> And I'm givin' the Devil reign
> 'Cause he's sinned, I got no choice
> It's run in my brain.

What then are the specific areas of conflict?

First, there is sexual temptation. Dylan writes in "Trouble in Mind":

> I got to know, Lord
> When to pull back on the reins
> Death can be the result of
> The most underrated pain.
>
> Satan whispers to ya
> 'Well I don't want to bore ya.
> But when you get tired of that Miss So-and-so
> I got another woman for ya.'

Next, there is the battle with his old self, his flesh. Dylan warns:

> It's the ways of the flesh
> To war against the spirit
> Twenty-four hours a day
> You can feel it, you can hear it.
> ("Solid Rock" on *Saved*)

Beyond this there is the battle with pride. (As C. S. Lewis points out, the sins of the spirit are more damning than the sins of the flesh.) It is always Satan who appeals to our self-glorification. Dylan writes of him:

> He's going to make you a law unto yourself
> Build a bird's-nest in your hair
> He's gonna deaden your conscience
> Till you worship the work of your hands
> You'll be serving strangers
> In a strange and forsaken land.
> ("Trouble in Mind")

Not only are there these internal battles, there is also the external battle, fought by those who no longer "fit" into the fallen world. Dylan writes of this in "Property of Jesus." First, he exposes the unbeliever's defensiveness toward the Christian who challenges his complacency.

> Go ahead and talk about him
> Because he makes you doubt
> Because he has denied himself
> The things you can't live without.
> (on *Shot of Love*)

Next, because of his surrender to Christ, the Christian can no longer be exploited. The world says he's "out of step with reality." The cause of this for Dylan is his liberation from Satan's bondage. He will be rejected, Dylan writes, "Because he doesn't pay tribute/To the king that you serve." Furthermore, the Christian is willing to take risks and no longer uses humor as a cover-up.

> Because he's not afraid of tryin'
> Say he's got no style
> 'Cause he doesn't tell you jokes or fairy tales
> Saints fail to make you smile.

Here we see Dylan's long-standing theme of being an outsider, out of the mainstream, given new power. He has written of outlaws, of John Wesley Harding, of Joey Gallo. He described Lenny Bruce as "the brother that you never had" ("Lenny Bruce" on *Shot of Love*). But this sense of alienation from the culture is now reborn in Christ. This deep moral and spiritual sense of not belonging is true. Dylan and all Christians are destined for heaven, for Augustine's "City of God," rather than for the city of man. For example, Malcolm Muggeridge speaks of going through life feeling like a "D.P.," a displaced person. When he finally became a Christian he discovered that this feeling of not belonging was a longing for God. As Dylan puts it in "Covenant Woman" on *Saved*, "You know that we are strangers/In a land we're passin' through." Alienation now is determined by a new sense of the final, heavenly goal.

The active Christian life, however, is not just negative, contending against the world, the flesh, and the devil. It also has its positive content—the call to love. Dylan asks:

> Am I ready to lay down my life for the brethren
> And to take up my cross
> Have I surrendered to the Word of God
> Or am I still acting like the boss?
> ("Are You Ready" on *Saved*)

For Dylan one summary of God's demand lies in the Golden Rule. Jesus says, "Do unto others as you would have them do unto you" (Matthew 7:12). Dylan interprets this command in "Do Right to Me, Baby." What he does not want for himself he will not do to others. He writes:

> Don't want to judge nobody
> Don't want to be judged
> Don't want to hurt nobody
> Don't want to be hurt.

He refuses to shoot, buy, or bury anybody, or marry anybody already married. He won't confuse, amuse, betray, or play with anybody. The point is in the chorus:

> But if you do right to me, Baby
> I'll do right to you, too.
> Got to do unto others
> Like you'd have them, like you'd have them
> Do unto you.
> (on *Slow Train Coming*)

It's as if, in rebuilding a Christian consciousness, after the "morals of despair," Dylan must take us back to basics and start over again.

So too, Dylan turns to the "love chapter," 1 Corinthians 13, for another exposition on how to live. In "Watered Down Love" he asserts that we don't want a pure love. To prove his point Dylan expounds on what pure love would be.

> Love that's pure
> Hopes all things
> Believes all things
> Won't pull no strings.
> (on *Shot of Love*)

Such a love won't engage in illicit sexual conquest. It won't make false claims. It intercedes rather than casting blame. He continues that such love

> Will not deceive you
> Lead you into trangression
> Won't write it up
> And make you sign a false confession.

It won't lead you astray, hold you back, get in your way. It's not envious or suspicious and is always content. It "never needs to be proud, loud/Or restlessly yearning."

Such a love then, takes the heart out of manipulation, selfishness, possessiveness—all of those things from which Dylan has fled in the past. Such a love can only be ultimately found in God's heart. In our egocentricity we want a "watered down love," but God gives us a pure love and renews our potential to love in this way.

A concrete example of Dylan's new perception of love is found in his expression of love for the opposite sex. Such love now stands within the covenant love he has received from God. Since God is its source, this love is enduring.

> Precious Angel
> You believe me when I say

What God has given to us
No man can take away.
("Precious Angel" on *Slow Train Coming*)

His woman now is a "Covenant Woman." He trusts her and will
be faithful to her trust. She is a sign of God's love: "He must
have loved me oh so much/To send me someone as fine as you"
("Covenant Woman" on *Saved*). They share intimacy and a common destiny. Dylan promises, "I'll always be right by your
side/I've got a covenant, too." Thus, their relationship is built on
God's gift rather than on romantic ideals which always disinte-
grate. Dylan will be a "Covenant Man" to his "Covenant
Woman."

In conclusion then, we see that the Christian life is lived by
the continuing grace of God; that is its "passive" side. This grace,
however, makes the believer active. He contends against God's
enemies and his own. He loves with a divine love that comes
from a heart renewed by grace, and his love becomes selfless because it is the very love of Christ in him. At the passive core, the
Christian lives by faith. But this faith propels him into God's
purpose. He participates in where history is going. He shares in
its ultimate outcome. To this we now turn.

The Final Resolution

The "train" on Dylan's *Slow Train Coming* is Jesus Christ.
Right now Christ is coming spiritually to people as He came to
Dylan. At the same time, Christ is yet to come in final glory.
Thus, the Christian lives between the First and Second Comings
of Christ. The final return of Christ, however, is determined by
His First Coming. As Dylan puts it, "What's to come has already
been" ('Pressin' On" on *Saved*). The future is controlled by the
incarnate Christ.

It is clear that much of Dylan's music and thinking is apocalyptic. Early in his career a song such as "When the Ship Comes
In" on *The Times They Are A-Changin'* denotes the final end to history with vindictive judgment. Even in his period of chaotic despair Dylan never lost touch with ultimate issues, although the
pictures he painted were full of darkness. With his conversion,
however, Dylan's sense of the apocalyptic was renewed. The
theme of warning still stands; but for Dylan, the future is now

resolved. The end will be neither by nuclear nightmare, nor by some other corruption (such as in "A Hard Rain's A-Gonna Fall") but by the hand of God.

Because Christ will return, all human plans for peace and security are futile. Dylan asks,

> Will I ever learn
> That there'll be no peace
> That the world won't cease
> Until He returns?
> ("When He Returns" on *Slow Train Coming*)

Human ideologies, political resolutions, the "politics of sin," manipulating Satan, all crumble before the mighty God. Dylan continues:

> Of every earthly plan
> That be known to man
> He is unconcerned.
>
> He's got plans of His own
> To set up His throne
> When He returns.

The return of Christ, then, is the cosmic, historical resolution for all the ambiguity, injustice, and chaos of this present age. The comprehensive social critique that Dylan offers in "Slow Train" is resolved by the "Slow Train coming 'round the bend," namely by Christ Himself. On that day Satan, sin, and death will all be vanquished and God's sovereignty and justice will be vindicated. As Dylan writes, "The strongest wall/Will crumble and fall to a mighty God" ("When He Returns" on *Slow Train Coming*).

The moral decay, so characteristic of our times, will also be reversed.

> Like a thief in the night
> He'll replace wrong with right
> When He returns.

Not only will there be a cosmic resolution, there will also be a personal resolution for Dylan. As he puts it in "Saving Grace":

> The death of life
> Then comes the resurrection
> Where I am welcome
> Is where I'll be.
>
> (on *Saved*)

Death is no longer the ultimate threat. In Christ's Resurrection Dylan is assured of his own resurrection and a welcome into God's presence.

In light of Christ's triumphant return, then, Dylan issues his evangelistic call. He warns, "Jesus said, 'Be ready/For you know not the hour which I come'" ("Gonna Change My Way of Thinking" on *Slow Train Coming*). While it is useless to set clocks and dates, we must be prepared. In "Are You Ready," Dylan writes:

> Are you ready to meet Jesus
> Are you where you want to be
> Will He know you when He sees you
> Or will He say, 'Depart from me'?
>
> (on *Saved*)

The decision for Christ made now determines our personal future.

> When destruction comes swiftly
> And there's no time to say, 'Fare-thee-well'
> Have you decided whether you wanta be
> In Heaven or Hell?

The future, determined by God, is clear. We, however, must answer the question Dylan poses:

> Are you ready for the judgment
> Are you ready for that terrible swift sword
> Are you ready for Armageddon
> Are you ready for the Day of the Lord?

Dylan pleads with us, "I hope you're ready." What then are we to make of this?

Mircea Eliade in *Cosmos and History* asserts that modern man

106

is "historical man." He consciously creates history. While the ancients fled from the evils of historical life into circular myths and rituals or escaped into some timeless state of being, we moderns are condemned to face the "terror of history." Why is this so? Our "realism" is the fruit of biblical faith.

In the Fertile Crescent, it was Israel alone who greeted raging armies, plagues, and natural disasters as bearing the hand of God. Rather than denying history, Israel saw history as the vehicle of God's work in judgment and redemption. For the Jews, the resolution of the "terror of history" lies in the final consummation of all things: the Messianic Age, the Day of the Lord. However secularized we may be today, we have inherited the biblical sense of history, and we look for meaning within it. Even in Marxism, history is not a succession of arbitrary accidents. It has a coherent structure and resolves the "terror of history" in a utopian classless society.

Thus, Dylan retains authentic biblical faith in looking for the Second Coming of Christ. He refuses to "demythologize" history by capitulating to an existentialist philosophy that posits meaning only in the subjectivity of one's own decisions or one's inward self. This is not merely because of some wooden sense of biblical authority. Dylan's confidence in Christ's return is grounded in the incarnation: "What's to come has already been." Furthermore, since Christ has resolved the personal issues of Dylan's struggle, He certainly will resolve the full range of historical and cosmic issues. If the end of history is not Christ, then not only is history meaningless, but Christ is less than adequate for all things. Some other ultimate, like nuclear catastrophy, interplanetary war, or ecological disaster, is more ultimate than Him. For the Christian this is unthinkable.

God is sovereign. The future is His as well as the past. "He has plans of His own/To set up His throne/When He returns." The only relevant question now is: "Are You Ready?"

Chapter 5—Warning

"I can smell something cooking
I can tell there's going to be a feast."

WITH *Infidels* Bob Dylan entered a new phase of his artistic career. As he said to Robert Hilburn, the time to tell people "how to get their souls saved" had passed for him. Dylan continued, "Now it's time for me to do something else...."[1]

For many critics that "something else" has meant Dylan's abandonment of his Christian faith. For example, Christopher Connelly advances this view in his *Rolling Stone* review of *Infidels*.[2] Connelly proposes that *Saved* and *Shot of Love* were the culmination of a process beginning with *Desire* where Dylan purged himself of the metaphors and personas that gave him "Sixties sainthood" through the honest exposure of his gutsy personal life. By becoming a Christian it was as if Dylan had "to adopt someone else's world view in order to replace the stream of figurative language that once coursed through him." Now all that is swept away. What is left is a forty-two-year-old man elegantly documenting his "world-weariness and frustration at the burdens of the past, but who, ... is singing in his chains like the sea." *Infidels*, for Connelly, is rooted "in an ineffably deep sadness." If Connelly is right, this album is a decisive break from the Slow Train period.

Although Hilburn also views *Infidels* as "generally secular," it is rooted in ideas, "And ideas are hurled at you in the album like pieces of a large, compelling puzzle." He continues, "The heart of [the] album is a series of critical yet compassionate looks

---

[1] Robert Hilburn, "Bob Dylan at 42—Rolling Down Highway 61 Again," *Los Angeles Times*, 30 Oct. 1983, Calendar, p. 3.
[2] Christopher Connelly, "Dylan Makes Another Stunning Comeback," *Rolling Stone*, Nov. 1983, p. 65–66.

at the state of the nation."[3] This seems to be supported by Dylan's own reasons for his song selection on *Infidels*. He talks with Hilburn about our perilous times: "That's the state of affairs right now. Maybe that's always been the state of affairs, but it seems especially true now. That's why I picked these particular songs for the album. I don't know if that (subject) appeals to people or not, but I felt I had to do these songs now."[4]

Social critique, however, has always been part of Dylan's repertory. The issue is whether that critique flows from his Slow Train period or simply picks up currents already present before his conversion. In other words, does *Infidels* stand in continuity with the immediate past or is it a decisive break from that past?

Before Connelly's and many other critics' conclusions are hastily embraced, it is well to note that in his interview given to Martin Keller in the summer of 1983 Dylan dropped a clue as to his present state of mind. He called *Shot of Love* (containing songs such as "Property of Jesus" and "Every Grain of Sand") his favorite album and the title song "my most perfect song." Dylan continued, "It defines where I am spiritually, musically, romantically and whatever else. It shows where my sympathies lie. No need to wonder if I'm this or that. I'm not hiding anything. It's all there in that one song. That's all you can ask."[5]

If Dylan is to be trusted here, and he is, then *Infidels* stands in direct continuity with *Shot of Love* and is in no way a break from the Slow Train period. In fact, *Infidels* can only be fully understood in the light of Dylan's Christian faith. What we have come to understand in the previous chapter about Dylan's "Vision" now opens up the depths of *Infidels*.

With *Infidels* Dylan returns to his interpretation of our times, but no longer is he asserting himself as an evangelist. Now, rather, his Christian message is guarded by parable and metaphor. In this respect, *Infidels* is more like *Slow Train Coming* than *Saved*. It has a prophetic stance.

The very title is illuminating. As we proposed in our intro-

---

[3] Robert Hilburn, "Dylan: The View From Route '84," *Los Angeles Times*, 5 Aug. 1984, Calendar, p. 54.
[4] Hilburn, "Bob Dylan at 42," p. 4.
[5] Martin Keller, "Dylan Speaks," *Us* magazine, 2 Jan. 1984, p. 59.

duction, the word *infidels*, at first glance, seems the opposite of faith. But is it? Who are these infidels? On the album itself they are all outsiders; they are those who are viewed foolish like "Jokerman." They are the "sweethearts like you" working in "a dump like this." They are the "Neighborhood Bully" who won't lie down and die. They are those who protest war and greed and violence. They are those who see through Satan's disguises when he comes as "a man of peace." In other words, the infidels are the *true* believers. They are those who have come to see the truth and who therefore challenge this world's system of deception.

The album cover features a full-face picture of Dylan hidden behind sunglasses, apparently driving in a car. It's as if the dividing line in the highway is reflected in his lenses. Here, a more guarded Dylan symbolizes his material. He is still on the road, but he will no longer come out with direct theological statements (except in "Man of Peace"). The glasses protect him, and at times we may have to see him ". . . through a glass, darkly . . ." (1 Corinthians 13:12).

Turning to the songs, the eight cuts reveal the terrain of this apocalyptic hour. The first side begins with a parabolic song to Christ. The second side begins with a literal song against Satan. The cosmic conflict, so characteristic of the Slow Train era, continues to determine reality for Dylan. We turn then to the theological content of the songs in the order in which they appear on *Infidels*.

"Jokerman"

As we have noted, Dylan begins *Infidels* with a song to Christ. Rather than the direct biblical exposition of "In the Garden" on *Saved*, Dylan creates a metaphor to slip Jesus by the censors who would turn him off before he can turn them on. In using the bold picture of Christ as "Jokerman," Dylan asserts the foolishness of the gospel to the world. Similarly, in his first letter to the Corinthians, Paul calls "Christ crucified" a stumbling block to the Jews and foolishness to the Gentiles (1:23).

"Jokerman" begins then with the Christ who, walking on the water (John 6:19), comes to cast the bread of His word before the false gods of this world:

> Standing on the waters, casting your bread
> While the eyes of the idol with the iron head are glowing.

Since Satan stands behind the idols (1 Corinthians 10:20), Christ is born strangling his snakelike representation.

> Distant ships sailing into the mist
> You were born with a snake
> In both your fists
> While a hurricane was blowing.

Christ, however, enters history for a moment and then escapes, leaving us with a question:

> Freedom just around the corner for you
> But with truth so far off, what good will it do?

Dylan answers this question with the chorus. In the midst of the darkness of this world, Christ dances to the song of the nightingale. Moonlight also beams the way to heaven for the birds who will follow it.

> Jokerman dance to the nightingale tune
> Bird fly high by the light of the moon
> Oh, — Oh, — Oh, — Jokerman.

Here is the moral and spiritual answer for those who have eyes to see and ears to hear.

Christ, however, is crucified after a brief ministry and then rises from the dead.

> So swiftly the sun sets in the sky
> You rise up and say good-bye to no one.

As the one who has conquered death, He does not experience the dread of the future. Like the snake, Christ sheds His skin as a sign of immortality and is always a step ahead of the devil.

> Fools rush in where angels fear to tread.
> Both of their futures, so full of dread, you don't show one
> Shedding off one more layer of skin
> Keeping one step ahead of the persecutor within.

Next, Christ goes to heaven from the mountain of ascension on a cloud (Acts 1:9). Rather than making our idle dreams come true, He shows us His truth.

> You're a man of the mountains, you can walk on the clouds
> Manipulator of crowds, you're a dream twister.

However, He is no mirage. He has really come into this world, but no one sunk in its corruption would want to be in His family.

> You're going to Sodom and Gomorrah
> But what do you care?
> Ain't nobody there
> Would want to marry your sister.

Nevertheless, Christ loves the outsiders—they are His people, not the nameless power brokers of this world.

> Friend to the martyr, a friend to the woman of shame
> You look into the fiery furnace, see the rich man without any name.

How are we to understand this "Jokerman"? Dylan says we should read the books of Leviticus, the Old Testament book of sacrifice, and Deuteronomy, the Old Testament book of Law. Jesus learned from them that He must obey God's will and offer Himself for the sins of the world:

> Well, the Book of Leviticus and Deuteronomy
> The law of the jungle and the sea are your only teachers.

Exalted to glory, then, Christ is both the coming, conquering King on a white charger depicted in the New Testament Book of Revelation (Revelation 19:11 ff.) and an intimate friend receiving the love of His creation.

> In the smoke of the twilight on a milk-white steed
> Michelangelo indeed could've carved out your features.
> Resting in the fields, far from the turbulent space
> Half asleep near the stars with a small dog licking your face.

Meanwhile, on this planet the sick and the lame are stalked by rifleman and preacherman, and "who'll get there first is uncertain." The world is gripped by violence, fear, and injustice. Dylan concludes:

> False-hearted judges dying in the webs that they spin
> Only a matter of time till night comes steppin' in.

But there is one more series of events before the end. In the Book of Revelation the Antichrist comes to lead the nations in their final rebellion against God. He is a prince, not a king, and is born by the scarlet woman, Babylon, the final world empire (Revelation 17:1-18).

> It's a shadowy world, skies are slippery grey
> A woman just gave birth to a prince today and dressed him in scarlet.

Capturing an apostate church (Revelation 13:11-18), the Antichrist persecutes the true church and brings the nations to commit spiritual fornication with Babylon the Great.

> He'll put the priest in his pocket, put the blade to the heat
> Take the motherless children off the street
> And place them at the feet of the harlot.

Christ, however, is not surprised by this turn of events. As we have seen, Antichrist has been prophesied in the Bible. So Dylan sings, "Oh, Jokerman, you know what he wants." Yet Christ's hand is never forced by Satan right up to the end: "Oh, Jokerman, you don't show any response." The chorus resolves the conflict; we are left with Christ dancing in the darkness to the nightingale's tune.

In this incredible barrage of images Dylan has captured the cosmic conflict, the majesty and mercy of Christ, our present perilous hour, and the final denouement with Antichrist yet to come. Here, once again, is Dylan's biblical world view establishing reality and offering salvation in the one whom the world cynically views as "Jokerman." All the rest of *Infidels* must be seen in relation to this foundational credo.

"Sweetheart Like You"

In the next cut, "Sweetheart Like You," Dylan moves from Christ to the Christian. The video Dylan made of this song was set in a café after closing time where a waitress was cleaning up. We are shown quickly however that the "dump like this" where she works is really the whole fallen world. In the song's first bridge Dylan warns of that world's temptation to fame and power. The picture suggests a rock star selling her soul:

> You know, you can make a name for yourself.
> You can hear them tires squeal.
> You can be known as the most beautiful woman
> Whoever crawled across cut glass to make a deal.

In the second bridge, Dylan observes that to be in a "dump like this" you have to be noted for the evil you've done, own women, and self-destruct on your musical genius.

> Got to be an important person to be in here, honey
> Got to have done some evil deed
> Got to have your own harem when you come in the door
> Got to play your harp until your lips bleed.

Finally, Dylan warns that the rulers of this world are thieves.

> Steal a little and they throw you in jail
> Steal a lot and they make you King.

The only thing worse than stealing votes is stealing souls by offering some spiritual Nirvana:

> There's only one step down from here, baby
> It's called the land of permanent bliss
> What's a sweetheart like you doin' in a dump like this?

As we have suggested the "Sweetheart Like You" is a Christian. She should be at home—out of the dump. Dylan awakens that longing, first of all, by simply asserting the need for a better life.

> You know, a woman like you should be at home
> That's where you belong
> Takin' care of somebody nice
> Who don't know how to do you wrong.

But beyond this longing is the reality of a heavenly Father and an eternal home. So Jesus tells His disciples, "In my Father's house are many mansions: if it were not so, I would have told you. I go to prepare a place for you. And if I go and prepare a place for you, I will come again, and receive you unto myself; that where I am, there ye may be also" (John 14:2, 3). Dylan reflects this:

> You know, news of you has come down the line
> Even before ya came in the door
> They say in your father's house, there's many mansions
> Each one of them got a fireproof floor.

Knowing her divine destiny, the sweetheart needs to be ready for rejection (similar thoughts have appeared in "I Believe in You" on *Slow Train Coming* and "Property of Jesus" on *Shot of Love*).

> Snap out of it, baby, people are jealous of you
> They smile to your face, but behind your back they hiss
> What's a sweetheart like you doin' in a dump like this?

If Christ is in conflict with Satan in "Jokerman," then the Christian is in conflict with the world in "Sweetheart Like You." The sweetheart is an "outsider," but it's not her problem. She's a sweetheart in a dump, destined for a better world to come.

"Neighborhood Bully"

In the next song, Dylan turns to another outsider, Israel, the "Neighborhood Bully." This rocking, driving song exposes the world's moral hypocrisy in dealing with the Jews. Now, back in their homeland at last, they are alone, fighting to survive. History, however, is on Israel's side:

> Every empire that's enslaved him is gone
> Egypt and Rome, even the great Babylon.

Moreover, the biblical prophecy that the Holy Land will bloom again (Deuteronomy 30:1, Isaiah 43:5; 49:8), is being fulfilled:

> He's made a garden of paradise in the desert sand
> In bed with nobody, under no one's command.

Enduring persecution, as promised in the Bible, the Jews have made miraculous strides.

> Now his holiest books have been trampled upon
> No contract he signed was worth what it was written on
> He took the crumbs of the world and he turned it into wealth
> Took sickness and disease and he turned it into health. . . .

This song has evoked high interest. Has Dylan shown his colors here? Is he a Zionist? Is he advocating political support for Israel? In a June 1984 interview for *Rolling Stone* Dylan denied being a political songwriter. He asserted, " 'Neighborhood Bully' to me, is not a political song. . . . It's simple and easy to define it, so you got it pegged, and you can deal with it in that certain kinda way. However, I wouldn't *do* that." He then cryptically suggested, "If you listen closely, it really could be about other things."[6] Indeed, the song is about other things as it concludes on a fully prophetic note.

According to the Bible the Jews' reoccupation of their land, their standing on the hill of Mount Zion, means that this age is now ending. After giving a catalog of final signs before His return, Jesus promised, "Truly I say to you, this generation will not pass away until all these things take place" (Mark 13:30 NAS). Thus, Dylan writes:

> Neighborhood bully standing on the hill
> Running out the clock, time standing still.

This is the apocalyptic moment. Antichrist is coming. The Jews are a nation again. The pieces fall into place for Armageddon as the prophetic clock ticks toward midnight.

"License to Kill"

The final cut on the first side of *Infidels*, "License to Kill," reveals man as a manipulated killer. Like Narcissus, he ends up by worshiping himself. Dylan laments this egotistic selfishness disguised as "freedom."

---

[6] Kurt Loder, "The Rolling Stone Interview: Bob Dylan," *Rolling Stone*, 21 June 1984, p. 17.

> Man thinks 'cause he rules the earth
> He can do with it as he please.

He warns:

> And if things don't change soon, he will.

And what man will do with the earth is simply destroy it. Why is this so?

To begin with, he is manipulated by the real power brokers of this world. They "groom him for life" which really means death. Trained to be a killer, he ends up being killed.

> Then they bury him with stars
> Sell his body like they do used cars.

Molded by his environment, man is "afraid and confused." His brain is "mismanaged." The world deceives him.

> All he believes are his eyes
> And his eyes, they just tell him lies.

Dylan's indictment, however, is not just against the world "out there." Man too is corrupt, absorbed in himself:

> Now he worships at an altar
> Of a stagnant pool
> And when he sees his reflection, he's fulfilled

consumed by selfishness,

> Oh, man is opposed to fair play
> He wants it all and he wants it his way.

Over against man, corrupted and corrupt, there is the haunting refrain:

> Now, there's a woman on my block
> She just sit there as the night grow still
> She say who gonna take away his license to kill?

Thus, Dylan brings side one of *Infidels* to its close by focusing down upon man himself, his moral responsibility, his ego-

tism, his violence, his license to kill. Rather than resigning himself to the way things are, however, Dylan demands intervention. The "License to Kill" must be revoked. But the human condition is not simply the result of man's rebellion and sin; the analysis goes deeper. This leads us to the first cut on side two.

"Man of Peace"

Dylan is now ready to introduce Satan himself in "Man of Peace." As we have already noted, it is only at this point that Dylan "tells it like it is." When talking about Satan, all parable and metaphor are jettisoned. Since the devil disguises himself as an angel of light (2 Corinthians 11:14), he must be called by name. Anything less would allow him to continue his deceptive ways.

In "Man of Peace" Dylan offers the most pointed warning on *Infidels*. Hilburn calls this the album's key song, and he is right.[7] Here Dylan's urgency breaks through. Satan's deceptions are found in the many disguises he adopts, the unknowing people he exploits, and the instinctive moves that he makes to attack our weaknesses.

In the first verse, Dylan summons us to watch a supposedly harmless scene. The band is playing; a speaker beckons to us. But it's lethal.

> Look out your window, baby
> There's a scene you'd like to catch.
> The band is playing "Dixie"
> A man got his hand outstretched.
> Could be the Führer, could be the local priest.
> You know, sometimes Satan comes as a man of peace.

Thus, Satan is a seducer. He has "a sweet gift of gab." He's smooth. He knows all the love songs ever sung. Dylan continues:

> Good intentions can be evil
> Both hands can be full of grease
> You know that sometimes Satan comes as a man of peace.

---

[7] Hilburn, "Bob Dylan at 42," p. 4.

Next, Satan moves quickly, unexpectedly.

> Well, first he's in the background, then he's in the front
>   Both eyes are looking like they're on a rabbit hunt.

The devil is the master of deception. Dylan asserts, "Nobody can see through him." Thus,

> He could be standing next to you
> The person that you'd notice least.

To get his way, he can either allure us or bore us to death.

> Well, he can be fascinating
> He can be dull.

Furthermore, because he is the great deceiver, even significant human "advances" can mask his evil work.

> He's a great humanitarian, he's a great philanthropist
>   He knows just where to touch you, honey,
>   And how you like to be kissed.
>   He'll put both his arms around you
> You can feel the tender touch of the beast.

Dylan now becomes urgent. This is the crisis, the apocalyptic hour. As we have seen, Antichrist is rising; Israel is running out the clock. Dylan warns:

> Well, the howling wolf will howl tonight, the king snake will crawl
>   Trees that've stood for a thousand years suddenly will fall.
>   Wanna get married? Do it now
>   Tomorrow all activity will cease. . . .

Dylan concludes with a most poignant picture: a mother weeping for her lost son. Where is her boy?

> . . . . he's following a star
> The same one them three men followed from the East.

Indeed, Satan does disguise himself as an angel of light. He can even use the same star that brought the wise men to Jesus.

Antichrist duplicates the miracles that Christ performed. In the Gospel of Mark, Jesus warns, "Many will come in My name, saying, 'I am He!' and will mislead many. . . . for false Christs and false prophets will arise, and will show signs and wonders, in order, if possible, to lead the elect astray" (Mark 13:6, 22 NAS).

In a time of great peril then, Satan comes as a "Man of Peace" offering a bogus security which is no peace. We should not be surprised at his message when the world careens on the brink of a nuclear holocaust. Satan would seduce us religiously, politically, and personally, promising "peace, peace," when there is no peace.

This song is the key to *Infidels* because it offers the basis for all the other warnings and presses home a sense of urgency. The hour is late; "do it now." "The howling wolf will howl *tonight*." As Dylan puts it:

> I can smell something cooking
> I can tell there's going to be a feast.

"Union Sundown"

Next, Dylan turns to the economic consequences of greed and the end of independent nations in one "global village." In "Union Sundown" the sun is going down on the union, namely the United States, the unions, and capitalism.

> Well, it's sundown on the union
> And what's made in the U.S.A.
> Sure was a good idea
> Till greed got in the way.

Our greed exploits the cheap labor of the Third World and destroys jobs at home. Dylan laments, "They don't make nothin' here no more." He continues:

> You know, capitalism is above the law
> It say, "It don't count 'less it sells."
> When it costs too much to build it at home
> You just build it cheaper someplace else.

124

It is our greed then that throws the nations into turmoil and builds the economic base for one interdependent world. In the June 1984 *Rolling Stone* interview Dylan commented on this, "Right now . . . there's a big push on to make a big global country—*one big country*—where you can get all the materials from one place and assemble them someplace else and sell 'em in another place, and the whole world is just all one, controlled by the same people, you know?"[8] This, again, paves the way for Antichrist's world rule (Revelation 13:16, 17).

If in "Union Sundown" Dylan gives the state of the nation, then in "I and I" he gives the state of his soul.

"I and I"

The title for this song employs the Rastafarian expression for "God and man." In the chorus Dylan speaks of himself in relation to God. He is the human "I" who stands before the divine "I." In God's presence he sees his own fallen state. At the same time, God veils Himself in His holiness as He speaks to us.

> I and I—One says to the other,
> No man sees my face and lives.

This last line comes from Exodus where Moses asks to see God's face and is refused. He is shown God's glory, but the Lord says to him, ". . . My face shall not be seen" (Exodus 33:23). The chorus then frames the ultimate issues; we live between our fallen nature and God's holiness: "No man sees my face and lives."

In these verses, Dylan begins with a sensual, romantic woman. Here is "mother earth," the feminine, drawing him in. Here is beauty, both seductive and idealized at the same time.

> Been so long since a strange woman
> Has slept in my bed.
> Look how sweet she sleeps
> How free must be her dreams.
>
> In another lifetime
> She must have owned the world

---

[8] Loder, "The Rolling Stone Interview: Bob Dylan," p. 18.

> Or been faithfully wed to some righteous king
> Who wrote psalms beside moonlit streams.

But Dylan abandons her. "Not much happenin' here, nothin' ever does." He turns from the beauty of romantic love to the question of his soul: "I and I"—he must live his life before God—that's reality.

Next, Dylan relates his conversion. Here he experiences a value reversal; now the winners are those who, in Paul's words, are diligent to present themselves "approved unto God, a workman that needeth not to be ashamed, rightly dividing the word of truth" (2 Timothy 2:15). Thus, Dylan writes:

> Took an untrodden path once
> Where the swift don't win the race
> It goes to the worthy
> Who can divide the word of truth.

It was Christ who, through His cross, taught Dylan that justice is real and wins out despite all the injustice in this world.

> Took a stranger to teach me,
> To look into justice's beautiful face
> And to see an eye for an eye
> And a tooth for a tooth.

The scene shifts—two men wait on the train platform "for spring to come, smoking down the track." The train is likely Christ's return: the "slow train comin' up around the bend" ("Slow Train"). The world's end, however, would not awaken the sleeping beauty, "She should still be there sleepin' when I get back."

Finally, Dylan pushes on in mid-life, "noontime." This is the "darkest part" and he can't stop: "I can't stumble or stay put." Whatever he says, it's his heart that must be heard, and while he has helped everyone, he himself still needs help.

> Someone else is speakin' with my mouth
> But I'm listening only to my heart.
> I've made shoes for everyone, even you,
> While I still go barefoot.

126

The song ends unresolved on one level. Dylan is barefoot. Yet the final resolution lies in the chorus, "I and I," the soul before God.

"Don't Fall Apart on Me Tonight"

On the most obvious level, the last cut on *Infidels*, "Don't Fall Apart on Me Tonight," is a pleading love song. In it Dylan asks his woman not to leave, but to stay and talk. It's a violent world out there and the past and the future don't exist. What the lovers have is each other now.

> Yesterday's just a memory
> Tomorrow is never what it's supposed to be.
> And I need you, yeah, yeah.

People pose a threat to them in an amoral age:

> Who are these people who are walking towards you?
> Do you know them or will there be a fight?
> With their humorless smiles so easy to see through
> Can they tell you what's wrong from what's right?

Dylan can't see this relationship going anywhere, yet he needs it and can't give it up. If he could, he would be different.

> I wish I'd have been a doctor
> Maybe I'd have saved some life that had been lost
> Maybe I'd have done some good in the world
> 'Stead of burning every bridge I crossed.

If he could he would take his woman to the mountaintop—but he's immobilized.

> But it's like I'm stuck inside a painting
> That's hanging in the Louvre
> My throat start to tickle and my nose itches
> But I know that I can't move.

What is left then? Simply to communicate: "Let's try to get beneath the surface waste, girl." If they can "hang in there" they

127

have a chance. Perhaps since they have a past, they can have a future.

> Yesterday's gone but the past lives on
> Tomorrow's just one step beyond
> And I need you, oh, yeah.

This is neither a song of passion nor of resignation. Neither is it heroic. It is a song of continuation—let's work on our relationship: "Do you think we can talk about it some more?"

As we noted before, this song poses as a love song. Yet on a deeper level it too may be parabolic. Does the woman represent Dylan's fans, the millions who have bought his records and heard his message? Is Dylan asking them not to fall apart on him or abandon him? Is he challenging them to "get beneath the surface waste" of this age? Is he reminding them of all he has said throughout his career because "the past lives on"? At the same time, is he expressing his frustration because he is stuck and cannot himself take them to the mountaintop? This sense of immobility is one of the major themes of *Infidels.* What then can we say overall about this album?

In the first place, the case has been made that *Infidels* is determined by Dylan's faith and stands organically linked to his Slow Train period. Here, however, he adopts a prophetic stance. This can be taken in two ways. In the classic sense, Dylan sees history climaxing according to the revealed, sovereign plan of God. Christ as "Jokerman," Satan as "Man of Peace," Antichrist as the scarlet prince, Israel as the "Neighborhood Bully"—all are the major movers of our times. This is to say, history is not, in Henry Ford's famous word, "Bunk"; history has meaning once we know the real forces behind it.

Dylan's work is also prophetic in the popular sense of addressing the moment. Here he is at his best. Dylan warns America of its greed in "Union Sundown." He exposes religious/political seduction in "Man of Peace." He attacks anti-Semitism in "Neighborhood Bully." He cautions against selling out in "Sweetheart Like You." He castigates violence and narcissism in "License to Kill."

Second, because *Infidels* is prophetic, Dylan continues to think "theologically" about life. His mind is structured by polarities:

Christ/Satan; the Christian/the world; Israel/the nations. For Dylan, Christ as "Jokerman" is the transcendent Lord who has come to fulfill Old Testament promises, to defeat Satan, the snake in both His fists, and to tear down our idols. He invades the corrupt world to befriend the martyrs and women of shame. In our darkness, He dances. In our despair, He celebrates.

Satan throws all his forces against Christ and tries to run off with the world. Through Antichrist he will martyr the church, put the blade to the heat, and give the masses to the great harlot, Babylon. At this moment, however, Satan continues his many disguises as the "Man of Peace." He makes his calculated moves, appeals to our weaknesses, slides in and out of our minds, and takes advantage of every situation turning it to himself.

His target is a lost humanity—man with his "License to Kill." Honored as he is slaughtered, bought and sold, destined for destruction, man in this world is the pragmatist who only believes his eyes—"And his eyes, they just tell him lies." What his eyes ultimately show him is only himself, and that is where he worships.

Because of man's killer instinct, our world is dangerous.

> Democracy don't rule the world
> You'd better get that in your head
> This world is ruled by violence.
> But I guess that's better left unsaid.
> ("Union Sundown")

Again:

> You know, the streets are filled with vipers
> Who've lost all ray of hope
> You know, it's not even safe no more
> In the palace of the Pope.
> ("Don't Fall Apart on Me Tonight")

Our greed also creates poverty which pushes the hungry of the world into more violence. And, again, that violence sets the stage for Satan's ruse as a "Man of Peace." In this sense, the world is being perfectly prepared for Antichrist to offer a false peace to the nations caught in such catastrophic turmoil. What we experience on a personal level, Israel is subject to on an international level. But this too, in God's sovereignty, is all a part of the plan to run out the clock of this historical period, leading to the establishment of His kingdom (see "When He Returns" on *Slow Train Coming*).

How then do we live in this world? Ask the question, "What's a sweetheart like you doing in a dump like this?" Remember the many mansions in your Father's house. Know that ultimately life is lived before God, "I and I." Take the "untrodden path" where the worthy "divide the word of truth." Be taught by the stranger who reveals justice's beautiful face. Have honest relationships; get below the surface. Here is the context of Dylan's theological thought.

Third, Dylan reveals himself in *Infidels* as frustrated about where history is and about where he is. It is this frustration that reviewers such as Connelly have responded to, and it bridges *Infidels* to Dylan's old fans and wider public.

He wishes he'd been a doctor and saved some lives rather than burning his bridges behind him. He's made shoes for everyone, but still goes barefoot. He feels like he's stuck inside a painting in the Louvre.

> My throat start to tickle and my nose itches
> But I know that I can't move.
> ("Don't Fall Apart on Me Tonight")

But these feelings are held in tension with a high degree of urgency that also pulses through the album. Dylan may be stuck for the moment but all will end soon. This is an apocalyptic hour.

> False hearted judges
> Dying in the webs that they spin.
> Only a matter of time
> Till night comes steppin' in.
> ("Jokerman")

Israel stands on the hill

> Running out the clock
> Time standing still.
> ("Neighborhood Bully")

Satan is ready to make his final move:

> Well, the howling wolf will howl tonight
> The king snake will crawl
> Trees that've stood for a thousand years
> Suddenly will fall.
> Wanna get married? Do it now
> Tomorrow all activity will cease.
> You know that sometimes Satan
> Comes as a man of peace.
> ("Man of Peace")

It is as if Dylan and time stand in the eerie quiet just before the storm. The cosmic conflict rages; the final resolution is sure. Meanwhile, our sense of being stuck is illumined by the moment in which we live before the end. But the end will come:

> I can smell something cooking
> I can tell there's going to be a feast.
> ("Man of Peace")

This is the prophet's warning. "He who has ears to hear, let him hear."

Chapter 6—Impact

*"I don't care how rough the road is
Show me where it starts."*

©1984 Los Angeles Times/Patrick Downs

W ITH our study of Bob Dylan completed, we may ask, What, then, is Dylan's contribution to our culture?

As we have already seen, it is difficult to overstate Dylan's impact upon his world. Michael Gray expresses it as follows, "By the beginning of the twenty-first century, and for a long time after that, those who want to understand the generations which grew up in the West in the 1960's–1980's will find it vital to study Bob Dylan's art closely."[1] It will be important, to be sure, to study his art, but not to the exclusion of his intellectual and spiritual odyssey. Jon Landau wrote in 1968 that Dylan was "one of the few intellectuals making popular music at this time. . . ."[2] The lyrics of the seventies and eighties make Landau's judgment current. Dylan is still one of the few intellectuals writing popular music.

Dylan has forced the mass culture of the West to face its options. That those options have been tested and found wanting is important not simply because Dylan is a rock superstar, but because Dylan is a thoughtful, intelligent human being. Although always sensing himself to be an alien, Dylan has not suffered from a lack of commitment. In fact, it has been within those commitments that the options, from political protest to romantic ecstasy, have been examined and found wanting. Dylan is not interested in the luxury of mere intellectual exchange. He is not "academic." As he responded to Jonathan Cott about his critics, "But my feelings come from the gut, and I'm not too con-

---

[1] Michael Gray, *The Art of Bob Dylan* (New York: St. Martin's Press, 1981), p. 7.
[2] Jon Landau, "John Wesley Harding," in *Bob Dylan: A Retrospective*, ed. Craig McGregor (New York: William Morrow, 1972), p. 259.

cerned with someone whose feelings come from his head. That don't bother me none."[3]

Dylan then serves us as a mirror. In his quest we see our quest. In his honesty we see our dishonesty. In his judgments we are judged. The masks, one by one, are dropped and we know it. It has been said of the Christian thinker C. S. Lewis that he left the twentieth century without an excuse. The same can be said of Dylan for the generations of the sixties to the eighties.

As we have seen, Dylan uses his razor-sharp intellect to challenge our age to examine its secular world view. In this he prepares the way for a fresh consideration of the biblical faith and its appeal to our hearts.

In a series of lectures given at Yale in 1931, historian Carl Becker pronounced the end to an eight-century-long process of abandoning the Christian framework of reality. In its place we now conceive of "existence as a blindly running flux of disintegrating energy." Becker uses an epigram of Aristophanes to sum up the modern mind: "Whirl is king, having deposed Zeus." Our modern cynicism often leading to despair is captured by Becker as he writes, "What is man that the electron should be mindful of him! Man is but a foundling in the cosmos, abandoned by the forces that created him. Unparented, unassisted and undirected by omniscient or benevolent authority, he must fend for himself, and with the aid of his own limited intelligence find his way about in an indifferent universe."[4]

Similar to Becker, Paul Johnson begins his history of the twentieth century, *Modern Times*, by asserting that relativity was one of the principal influences on our age because it was used to cut society free from the faith and morals of our Judeo-Christian culture. The collapse of what Johnson calls "the religious impulse" left a huge vacuum. Faith was replaced by secular ideology and Nietzsche's Will to Power produced a new kind of Messiah in Hitler and Stalin "uninhibited by any religious sanctions whatever, and with an unappeasable appetite for controlling mankind. The end of the old order, with an unguided world

---

[3] Jonathan Cott, "Bob Dylan, 1978," in *The Rolling Stone Interviews* (New York: St. Martin's Press/Rolling Stone Press, 1981), p. 363.
[4] Carl Becker, *The Heavenly City of the Eighteenth-Century Philosophers* (New Haven: Yale University Press, 1932), p. 15.

adrift in a relativistic universe, was a summons to such gangster-statesmen to emerge."

If "Whirl is king" then the march of the dictators is the political consequence of Whirl. But the deeper possibility is that Whirl is Satan and the march of the dictators sets the stage for his final apocalpyse in the coming of Antichrist. Why then would Dylan follow the Bible rather than Whirl? There is a twofold answer to this question. First, Dylan did follow Whirl for years and it led him nowhere; he simply ended with the "morals of despair." Second, Dylan was finally confronted by what William James called "irreducible brute facts" that cleared his mind and healed his heart. The modern world would like to forget these facts, but they stand at the very foundation of our civilization: the biblical revelation of God's purpose in history through Israel climaxing in Jesus Christ. Not only was there the biblical revelation, there was also the risen Christ. As we have seen, Dylan describes "this *vision* and *feeling*" when his room moved and "there was a presence in the room that couldn't have been anybody but Jesus."

Out of this encounter then, Dylan began to tell the gospel story once again. With deep conviction, a strong theology, and an open vulnerable heart, Dylan confessed his faith through his gospel tours and albums. Such candor must be honored. To write Dylan off as a "Fundamentalist" and not to hear him would be a tragic loss.

Malcolm Muggeridge warns of the terrible destruction of words in our time. As we lose the meaning of words, we are helpless and defenseless. In *The End of Christendom* he writes, "For instance, we speak of liberalizing our abortion laws, which means simply facilitating more abortion. Or we speak of reforming our marriage laws, when we mean creating facilities for breaking more and more marriages." Dylan can help us here. He is a master of words, and they are like arrows aimed at our hearts. Listening to him will make us honest. We will be helped to clean up our own communication.

Moreover, the gospel story is not merely an exercise in clear concepts. It is the story of God's heart to the human heart. For this reason, Dylan is able to tell it better than most working theologians. William Blake writes:

This life's dim Windows of the Soul
Distorts the Heavens from Pole to Pole
And leads you to believe a Lie
When you see with, not thro' the eye.

Dylan, like Blake, sees "thro' the eye." In *Jesus: The Man Who Lives* Muggeridge observes, "It is commentators like Blake and Tolstoy, Simone Weil, and Dostoevski, who preeminently bring Jesus to life, because they approach him through the imagination as artists rather than through the intellect as theologians."

To tell the gospel requires both the intellect and the emotions, the mind and the heart. Here Dylan brings the gift of brilliance, employing the power of poetry controlled by the discipline of meter and measure, engaging us as total persons. When we hear Dylan, our minds are focused, our emotions soar, our bodies begin to move to the music, and we are caught up together in the Divine Drama.

Dylan's "post-modern" confession then stands as a formidable intellectual challenge to our age. Dylan, however, is not chiefly concerned with the mind. His focus is on the heart, and here he has made a virtually unequaled contribution to our understanding of authentic spirituality. The roots of this understanding are dug deeply into the Bible itself. The literature of the heart begins with the Apostle Paul as he writes, "I count everything as loss because of the surpassing worth of knowing Christ Jesus my Lord . . ." (Philippians 3:8 RSV).

Classic witnesses to the regenerated heart continue with Augustine's *Confessions*. In A.D. 386 in a little garden in Milan, Augustine writes, "I probed the hidden depths of my soul and wrung its pitiful secrets from it, and when I mustered them all before the eyes of my heart, a great storm broke within me, bringing with it a great deluge of tears." Seizing upon Paul's letter to the Romans, he read from chapter 13. Then Augustine recalls, "I had no wish to read more and no need to do so. For in an instant . . . it was as though the light of confidence flooded into my heart and all the darkness of doubt was dispelled."

Perhaps the nearest literary expression to Dylan's conversion is found in Pascal. His handwritten statement was found sewn into his clothing at the time of his death in 1662 at thirty-nine years of age. Malcolm Muggeridge describes it as an "intensely moving document which like some spiritual seismograph reflects in its very strokes and flourishes the fluctuations of his state of mind as he was writing it."[5] At the top of the paper was a tiny cross followed by the date. Then the word *fire* appeared, signifying "the God of Abraham, the God of Isaac, the God of Jacob" but not "the God of the philosophers and scholars." Pascal continued, "Certainty, certainty, emotion, joy, peace, God of Jesus Christ. *DEUM MEUM ET DEUM VESTRUM*, Thy God shall be my God. Oblivion of the world and of everything except God." "Joy, joy, tears of joy."

So, over three hundred years later, in "Every Grain of Sand" (on *Shot of Love*), Bob Dylan writes:

> In the time of my confession
> In the hour of my deepest need
> When the pool of tears beneath my feet
> Floods every new born seed.
>
> There's a dying voice within me
> Reaching out somewhere
> Toiling in the danger
> And in the morals of despair.

As we have seen in chapter 3, with truth and grace, Dylan takes us to the consummation of that hour. His description bears repeating as he shows his eyes opening.

> In the fury of the moment
> I can see the Master's hand
> In every leaf that trembles
> In every grain of sand.

His moral struggle, however, is not over. He continues:

> I gaze into the doorway
> Of temptation's angry flame
> And every time I pass that way
> I always hear my name.

---

[5] Malcolm Muggeridge, *The Third Testament* (Boston: Little, Brown, 1976), p. 65.

But the hand of the Creator now rests upon him.

> Then onward in my journey
> I come to understand
> That every hair is numbered
> Like every grain of sand.

He then chronicles the Divine pursuit, revealing the ambivalence of his own heart.

> I hear the aged footsteps
> Like the motion of the sea
> Sometimes I turn, there's Someone there
> Othertimes, it's only me.

The final verse picks up the theme of the first verse.

> I am hanging in the balance
> Of the 'Reality of Man'
> Like every sparrow fallin'
> Like every grain of sand.

Such self-revelation, such honesty and intensity belong to classical spiritual literature. As Dylan makes his contribution he joins a highly select company.

Dylan has also added to the literature of devotion. "I Believe in You" on *Slow Train Coming* witnesses to a vital faith dealing with suffering and rejection. Like many of David's Psalms, the confessional part of the poem

> And I, I walk out on my own
> A thousand miles from home
> But I don't feel alone
> 'Cause I believe in you

turns to prayer:

> Don't let me drift too far
> Keep me where you are
> Where I will always
> Be renewed.

The prayer then returns to confession.

> And what you have given me today
> Is worth more than I can pay
> And no matter what they say
> I believe in you.

"What Can I Do For You" on *Saved* is a prayer that centers in the confession of God's absolute grace.

> You have given everything to me
> What can I do for you?

Dylan continues:

> You have given all there is to give
> What can I give for you?
> You have given me life to live
> How can I live for you?

The rhetorical questions bear their own answer, but Dylan ends on a ringing affirmation:

> I don't care how rough the road is
> Show me where it starts
> Whatever pleases you
> Tell it to my heart.

Another prayer-song speaks of God's complete grace and forgiveness in a profoundly personal way.

> If you find it in your heart can I be forgiven?
> Guess I owe you some kind of apology.
> I've escaped death so many times, I know I'm only livin'
> By the saving grace that's over me.
>
> By this time I'd thought that I'd be sleepin'
> In a pine box for all eternity
> My faith keeps me alive, but I still be weepin'
> For the saving grace that's over me.
> ("Saving Grace" on *Saved*)

141

Along with the literature of the heart, there is the literature of the conscience. In his prophetic stance, Dylan does what Amos, Isaiah, and Jeremiah did so long ago in Israel. Like these earlier mouthpieces for God, because Dylan loves his country, he can address her sins with so much passion. We have already covered the scope of his complaint. In "Slow Train," Dylan exposes the insult of the energy crisis, the arrogance and stupidity of "big-time negotiators," the national selfishness of hoarding food, the politics of absurdity: "trying to manipulate Satan," religious hucksters, and the ultimate insult of turning people into puppets.

When the president promises us renewed plenty, we don't like to hear that our grain elevators are bursting while the world starves. In the post-Watergate Era, we forget easily that lawbreakers are making the rules. In our highly urbanized, technological culture where the nation is glued to the TV screen, we don't want to believe that our loved ones are manipulated mannequins. Yet all of this is happening in front of our eyes.

At the same time, we don't want Dylan to burst our liberal bubble. We prefer Pete Seeger's optimistic humanism to Dylan's dark picture of human history and the human heart. As we go again into the streets to ban the bomb, we don't want Dylan to tell us that there will be no peace "until He returns." We don't want to be reminded of

> Drought and starvation
> Packaging of the soul
> Persecution, execution
> Governments out of control.
> ("Trouble" on *Shot of Love*)

We don't want to think seriously about even the existence of the devil, much less his disguise as a "Man of Peace." As Camus observes, we still forget to be modest.

Most of all, we don't want to know the deceptiveness of our own hearts. Dylan is too candid, too revealing. He asks:

> How long can I listen to the lies of prejudice
> How long can I stay drunk on fear
> Out in the wilderness?

We don't want to be probed by these questions. He continues:

> Can I cast it aside
> All this loyalty and this pride
> Will I ever learn?
> ("When He Returns" on *Slow Train Coming*)

A particular focus of Dylan's cultural critique is the media. This is true not only because he is a part of that industry, but also because of its pervasive power over our lives. In the interview given to Martin Keller in the summer of '83 Dylan talks first about the banality of modern journalism. He asserts that "most people's sensibilities are determined by the newspaper they read this morning, whether it be the *New York Daily News* or *The Wall Street Journal*. It's all the same. They cut down trees to print them all. What's the difference? It's doing nothing to get you into the world to come. No small wonder everyone's walking about insane."[6]

Next, Dylan takes on the economic exploitation of music: "When you go into a department store to buy an umbrella, your mind is attacked by fictitious sound—the B-52s, the Pretenders or somebody—and you kind of end up drifting in and out while the cash registers ring." Dylan warns against this corruption: "I don't remember that being the purpose of music. The purpose of music is to elevate the spirit and inspire. Not to help push some product down your throat."

While in Europe in '84 Dylan intensified his critique: "We're constantly being bombarded by insulting and humiliating music, which people are making for you the way they make those Wonder Bread products. . . . Just as food can be bad for your system, music can be bad for your spiritual and emotional feelings. It might taste good or clever, but in the long run it's not going to do anything for you."[7]

Previously, Dylan has discussed his own motive for his music. In his London radio interview of 1981 he says, "I just have to hope that in some kind of way this music that I've always

[6] Martin Keller, "Dylan Speaks," *Us* magazine, 2 Jan. 1984, pp. 58-59.
[7] Robert Hilburn, "Dylan: The View From Route '84," *Los Angeles Times*, 5 Aug. 1984, Calendar, p. 54.

played is a healing kind of music. I mean if it isn't I don't want to do it, because there's enough . . . so-called music out there which is sick music. It's just sick. It's made by sick people, and it's played to sick people to further a whole world of sickness."

Thus, pop music has become one "Rocky Horror Show." The despair of the beat generation of the fifties and the hippies of the sixties is the anarchy of the punk rockers and "new wavers" in the eighties. But even the mainstream of rock music reflects that anarchy, symbolized in Mick Jagger's leer as easily as in the Sex Pistols or Culture Club. When Dylan sings of the "Nightclubs of the brokenhearted/Stadiums of the damned" ("Trouble" on *Shot of Love*), both the musicians and their audiences are there.

Moreover, Dylan sees this sickness not only in rock 'n' roll. It is throughout the media. He continues, "Now this is not only true of music, this is true in the film industry. This is true in the magazine industry. Certainly it's a lot . . . on television, billboard signs. You know it caters to people's sickness."

What role then does Dylan see himself playing in the culture? He responds, "If I can't do something that is tellin' people—or hopin' anyway—that they . . . whatever their sickness is, and we're all sick, whatever it is . . . ah . . . you can be healed and well and set straight. Well if I can't do that, I'd just as soon be on a boat. . . ."

Dylan stands before the culture then, not only as a prophet to denounce its ills, but also as a priest to offer it healing. That healing is love, God's love. Again, Dylan says to Jonathan Cott, "Love comes from the Lord—it keeps all of us going. If you want it, you got it."[8] It is as a witness to God's healing love then that Dylan now marshalls his poetic genius, prophetic honesty, biblical depth, and cultural relevance. There are few people today who can equal his power both in what he says and how he says it.

There is no doubt that Dylan's spiritual contribution through his poetry is now substantial and enduring. Some of his writing, especially dealing with his conversion, is almost peerless. Other songs bear deep devotional insight and prophetic

---

[8] Cott, in *The Rolling Stone Interviews*, p. 359.

power. One day it may be that Dylan will be the classical standard for his art form as Bach and Handel are for theirs. For this to happen, however, Dylan would have to gain access to and appreciation from the institutional church. This, however, will not be easy.

Because Dylan became a Christian as an established artist and as a mature man committed to getting to the root of things, he has no entangling alliances. This gives him the freedom to speak the truth as he sees it and to unmask hypocrisy where he finds it. He also has the freedom that few clergymen find in their own pulpits to deal with the sins of our culture.

Dylan is not afraid of rejection. He is willing to suffer. He knows what it is to be booed. His goal is not to please people. He gave that up long ago. Thus, he has a personal integrity that is admirable. He prays:

> I don't care how rough the road is
> Show me where it starts
> Whatever pleases you
> Tell it to my heart.
> ("What Can I Do For You" on *Saved*)

What then are Dylan's possibilities for moving the culture in the eighties as he did in the sixties? At first glance they may seem minimal. Each generation has its own music. Dylan is now in his forties. Will youth even identify with him in a major way? Since Dylan's output is in a clearly spiritual direction, doesn't this limit his market?

In the first flush of Dylan's going public after his conversion, he refused to sing his older songs. Launching off on his gospel tour and battered by the media, Dylan later found empty seats in his concert halls. While *Slow Train Coming* went platinum, *Saved* and *Shot of Love* failed even to make gold.

As we noted, however, Dylan then began to mix the old songs with the new. This, as we have seen, was a necessary step in his own growth. At the same time, Dylan's writing moved beyond a narrow evangelistic mode. Thus, with the release of *Infidels*, the spiritual message is now in parables. At the same time, here is protest, cutting and clear. Here is warning about satanic seduction. Here is the setup for the apocalyptic end of the age.

And all of this is bridged to us with a tension between personal frustration and urgent appeal.

The commercial success of *Infidels* reveals that Dylan cannot be counted out of a major continuing role in the culture. He towers in sheer creative genius. This is not only true of his records but also of his concerts.

Dylan's impact will continue to be measured in part by the energy he is willing to put into touring. As long as he personally takes his music to the public, he will have a public. Jon Landau wrote, "Dylan is one of the finest singers of rock-and-roll who ever lived. . . ."[9] This judgment was made in 1968. Eleven years later, Jann Wenner, in *Rolling Stone* said: "Bob Dylan is the greatest singer of our times. No one is better. No one, in objective fact, is even very close. His versatility and vocal skills are unmatched. His resonance and feeling are beyond those of any of his contemporaries. More than his ability with words, and more than his insight, his voice is God's greatest gift to him."[10]

Jonathan Cott asks Dylan why he continues to do concerts. He replies, "Actually, it's all I know how to do. Ask Mohammed Ali why he fights one more fight. Go ask Marlon Brando why he makes one more movie. Ask Mick Jagger why he goes on the road. . . . Is it so surprising I'm on the road? What else would I be doing in this life, meditating on the mountain? Whatever someone finds fulfilling, whatever his or her purpose is—that's all it is."[11] Clearly, Dylan's identity and vocation are in making music before a live audience.

Sam Shepard describes the experience of Dylan in concert this way: "When he's up there. When he's free to work his magic. No one can touch him. . . . Who is he anyway? What kind of person moves like that? Stiff necked from his harmonica brace. Alternate rocking side to side. Keeping equal time on each foot. . . . Dancing backward into black space. . . . Re-emerging. Arriving at the mike at the very last fraction of a second. At a moment when any other performer on earth would have already

[9] Landau, "John Wesley Harding," in *Bob Dylan: A Retrospective*, p. 255.
[10] Jann Wenner, "Bob Dylan and Our Times: The Slow Train Is Coming," *Rolling Stone*, 20 Sept. 1979, p. 95.
[11] Cott, in *The Rolling Stone Interviews*, p. 357.

blown it. But now he's minus guitar. Has he lost it? . . . What's he got in his hand? Then, wham, it's on them before the shock can even register. Harmonica cuts the air like his phantom brother. He adds it like a character to a play. The audience is busted. Their skulls can't take it. The harp sound is awesome in its lonely courage. It cuts into every single soul within earshot. It takes the roof right off and sends this massive human chemistry flying out into the freezing night. . . . Here is the magician. Before their eyes. . . . It's the heart all along that we're searching for and now he's shown them to it by a sleight of hand. A flash of chrome between his teeth."[12]

Once *Infidels* had climbed the charts, Dylan gave a cover interview to *Rolling Stone* and launched a summer tour to Europe. Starting in Verona, Italy, he played twenty-five dates in less than two months, joined by Santana and a changing cast of notables including Joan Baez.

The tour was an unequivocable success. It was to Europe what the '84 Jacksons' tour was to the United States. Reported extensively in the media, Dylan played to 72,000 fans in Paris, 50,000 in Ireland (the biggest concert of the year there), and another 72,000 in London. *Rolling Stone* reported that the London concert was one of the highlights of Dylan's performing career and that he looked like "a holy man possessed." There he sang twenty-five songs, including three from *Infidels* and "Every Grain of Sand."

Bob Dylan told Jonathan Cott, "The Seventies I see as a period of reconstruction after the Sixties, that's all. That's why people say: 'Well, it's boring, nothing's really happening,' and that's because wounds are healing. By the Eighties, anyone who's going to be doing anything will have his or her cards showing. You won't be able to get back in the game in the Eighties."[13] Whatever his personal struggles, Dylan's cards are clearly showing. He is in the game. Forces beyond his control will determine the impact of his play.

In conclusion, Dylan comes to us, with, in Jann Wenner's phrase, "a transcendent and cohesive vision." It is cohesive be-

---

[12] Sam Shepard, *Rolling Thunder Logbook* (New York: Penguin Books, 1977), p. 79.
[13] Quoted in Alan Rinzler, *Bob Dylan: The Illustrated Record* (New York: Harmony Books, 1978), p. 120.

cause it shows history grounded in the divine purpose, and coming to its consummation in the divine plan.

As we have seen, Dylan refuses to "demythologize" history. He is unwilling to surrender his cohesive vision to the powers of fragmentation and chaos, reducing the fortress of truth to the rubble of opinion. He doesn't offer how-to tips for emotional well-being or financial success. Dylan's message is integrating rather than disintegrating as he catches us up into the ultimate destiny toward which we all are moving and being moved.

In an apocalyptic age, Dylan gives us the true apocalypse, the unveiling. No longer does he see "six crooked highways," "seven sad forests," or "a dozen dead oceans":

> Where the people are many and their hands are all empty,
> Where the pellets of poison are flooding their waters,
>
> . . . . .
>
> Where the executioner's face is always well hidden,
> Where hunger is ugly, where souls are forgotten. . . .
>
> ("A Hard Rain's A-Gonna Fall" on
> *The Freewheelin' Bob Dylan*)

Nor does he flee into silence behind the "Gates of Eden."

For Dylan, it is Jesus Christ who stands at the end of history. The nations are accountable to His final judgment, to behold His glory throughout the planet.

Each of Dylan's recent albums contains this apocalyptic theme. "When He Returns" closes *Slow Train Coming.* As we have seen, this song is filled with sober truth and evangelical passion. Here Dylan's "transcendent and cohesive vision" reveals God's sovereign power.

> The strongest wall
> Will crumble and fall
> To a mighty God.

Dylan softly pleads:

> Don't you cry
> And don't you die
> And don't you burn.

and warns:

> Like a thief in the night
> He'll replace wrong with right
> When He returns.

On *Saved* Dylan concludes with "Are You Ready." He asks:

> Are you ready for the judgment
> Are you ready for that terrible swift sword
> Are you ready for Armageddon
> Are you ready for the Day of the Lord?

Dylan closes *Shot of Love* with two songs. "Trouble" sets the scene of universal disaster. Then Dylan follows with his conversion as the answer in "Every Grain of Sand." While overtly less apocalyptic, this song demonstrates Dylan's personal deliverance from the microcosm of despair reflected elsewhere in the macrocosm of universal chaos. So he concludes:

> I am hanging in the balance
> Of the 'Reality of Man'
> Like every sparrow falling
> Like every grain of sand.

On *Infidels*, Dylan ends "Jokerman" with the closing of this age from the Book of Revelation:

> It's a shadowy world, skies are slippery grey
> A woman just gave birth to a prince today and dressed him in scarlet.
> He'll put the priest in his pocket, put the blade to the heat
> Take the motherless children off the street
> And place them at the feet of a harlot.

"Neighborhood Bully" also concludes with Israel in position for the end of the world, "running out the clock," and Dylan warns in "Man of Peace":

> Wanna get married? Do it now
> Tomorrow all activity will cease.

The cosmos, the nations, the whole of humanity, and each heart hang in the balance. It is only such a "transcendent and cohesive vision" that can keep us through this hour of peril and trial.

Chapter 7—Epilogue

*"He's got plans of His own
To set up His throne
When He returns."*

©1978 Wide World Photos

D URING World War II, after the fall of France, British Intelligence positioned "stay-behind spies" in Nazi occupied territory. Their role was to merge into the culture until the time when they would be called upon to monitor enemy troop movements for England. Analogously, Malcolm Muggeridge proposes that in each critical historical epoch God has had His stay-behind spies, such as Augustine when Rome was falling, Pascal when rationalism created the modern age, Tolstoy when dialectical materialism descended upon the Soviet people, and Bonhoeffer when Hitler took the mantle of an antichrist in his thousand-year *Reich*. Muggeridge writes, "I came to see them as God's spies, posted in actual or potential enemy-occupied territory. The enemy being, of course, in this particular case, the Devil."[1] Is not Bob Dylan in our time another of God's stay-behind spies?

Imbedded in the culture, commanding intellectual and artistic brilliance, a hero of mythic proportions, Bob Dylan uniquely communicates to a world molded by the media. His albums are racked in record stores literally around the world. His songs are aired in every major English-speaking metropolitan area. He unmasks us by unmasking himself, driving us to the ultimate spiritual questions.

In certain respects Bob Dylan is to our world what Augustine was to his. Both lived in a time of massive cultural dislocation and decay. Both rejected Christianity in an earlier period of their lives. Both were men of letters—Augustine with his rhetoric, Dylan with his poetry. Both exhausted their cultural alternatives and came up empty-handed. Both were haunted by

---

[1] Malcolm Muggeridge, *The Third Testament* (Boston: Little, Brown, 1976), p. 14.

absolutes. As Augustine confesses, if he had not known the immutable he could not have known that it was preferable to the mutable. "And so, in an instant of awe, my mind attained to the sight of the God who *is*."[2] Both rejected the external world and turned inward. Both experienced a dramatic conversion. Both communicated their conversion in intensely personal ways, opening their hearts to the world. Both suffered rejection for their faith. Both became prominent in their time.

Peter Brown attributes to Augustine the "hallmark of a genius." He writes, "Augustine possesses the relentless ability to work out in precise and cogent detail, an intuition that had already been hovering in a partial, confused form, at the back of the minds of his contemporaries."[3] The same is true of Bob Dylan. With uncanny intuition, in Sam Shepard's word with his "magic," Dylan verbalizes the inarticulate demands, longings, fears, and hopes of a generation.

As was earlier mentioned, before Dylan left for his European tour in the summer of '84 he granted a rare interview to *Rolling Stone*. The cover picture shows him staring intently into the camera with his chin resting on his fist, a thoughtful pose. Inside, the interview is also the lead story. What then are some major points that Dylan makes?

First of all, Dylan affirms a transcendent meaning to life. When asked about his "spiritual stance" he replies, "Well, I don't think that *this is it*, you know—this life ain't nothing."[4] Later he elaborates: "If you believe in *this* world, you're stuck; you really don't have a chance. You'll go *mad*, 'cause you won't see the end of it. You may wanna stick around, but you won't be able to. On another level, though, you *will* be able to see this world. You'll look back and say, 'Ah, that's what it was all about all the time. Wow, why didn't I *get* that?' " While still refusing the label "born again" as a media term, Dylan insists that there is a world to come, "that no soul has died, every soul is alive, either in holiness or in flames."

Second, Dylan reaffirms the biblical basis for his faith. He

---

[2] Peter Brown, *Augustine of Hippo* (Berkeley: University of California Press, 1967), p. 96.
[3] Ibid., p. 153.
[4] Kurt Loder, "The Rolling Stone Interview: Bob Dylan," *Rolling Stone*, 21 June 1984, p. 17.

claims to be a "literal believer of the Bible." When asked if both Old and New Testaments are equally valid, he answers, "To me." The interviewer later asks if Dylan is willing to talk to Orthodox Jews about Christianity. He responds, "Well, yeah, if somebody asks me, I'll tell 'em. But, you know, I'm not gonna just offer my opinion. I'm more about playing music, you know?"

Dylan especially singles out the importance of one biblical book. "I believe in the Book of Revelation. The leaders of this world are eventually going to play God, if they're not *already* playing God, and eventually a man will come that everybody will think *is* God. He'll do things, and they'll say, 'Well, only God can do those things. It must be him!'"

As we have seen, *Infidels* is an album of warning determined by biblical apocalyptic. When Dylan talks about Israel in the context of "Neighborhood Bully," he remarks in the interview that the present political situation in the Middle East won't last. He then continues, "The battle of Armageddon is specifically spelled out; where it will be fought, and, if you wanna get technical, *when* it will be fought. And the battle of Armageddon definitely will be fought in the Middle East." Then revealing the thought behind "Man of Peace," Dylan declares that politics "is an instrument of the Devil." Through our communications systems the world is becoming one "global people." This, as we have seen, prepares for Antichrist. So, Dylan continues, "We're thinkin' in terms of the whole world because communications come right into your house. Well, that's what the Book of Revelation is all *about*. And you can just about *know* that anybody who comes out for peace is *not* for peace." Dylan later brings up our global economic interdependence as also preparing for the end. As we have already seen this is addressed in "Union Sundown."

Dylan, however, is no fanatic announcing that "the end is at hand." He speculates that we may have another two hundred years. The new kingdom will come, but "people can't even imagine what it's gonna be like."

Throughout the interview Dylan never talks directly about Jesus. But the man who wrote the cryptic "Jokerman" as the lead song on *Infidels* will now guard himself against all the public abuse he received in his Slow Train period. At one point, however, the interviewer asks Dylan about his best friend. Dylan laughs with perhaps some discomfort: "My best friends? Jeez, let me try to think of one." Pressed he responds, "Best friends? Jesus, I mean that's. . . ." He is then cut off: "You've got to have a best friend," the interviewer insists. Finally, Dylan replies, "Well, there *has* to be . . . there *must* be . . . there's *gotta* be. But hey, you know, a best friend is someone who's gonna die for you. I mean, that's your best friend, really."

At first reading, it looks like Dylan uses *Jesus* in a profane way. On second reading, however, it is right at the point of struggling with the question about his best friend that Dylan speaks the name Jesus, and then goes on to identify a best friend as one who "dies for you." The poet's double intention is clear. As Jesus tells His disciples the night before the cross, "Greater love has no one than this, that one lay down his life for his friends" (John 15:13 NAS). Dylan is "Pressin' On." He doesn't look back.

Does Dylan again lead the pack standing on the edge of a major spiritual awakening in the West? Or will he merely go through another phase and then move on to other options as he has done in the past? By his own admission, "The Devil's shining light/It can be most blinding."

In this study, we have seen, however, that Dylan became a thoroughly converted man. Whatever course his life takes, he will be unable to escape that "vision and feeling" when he knew that the presence of Jesus was in his room.

What will the future hold? Dylan's answer to this final question carries an ambiguity informed by his faith. "My ways are not your ways," saith the Lord.

> Of every earthly plan
> That be known to man
> He is unconcerned.
> He's got plans of His own
> To set up His throne
> When He returns.
> ("When He Returns" on *Slow Train Coming*)

Millions upon millions of people would agree. None would say it better than Bob Dylan.

Bibliography

Augustine. *Confessions.* New York: Penguin Books, 1961.

Becker, Carl. *The Heavenly City of the Eighteenth-Century Philosophers.* New Haven: Yale University Press, 1932.

"Bob Dylan: His Born-Again Show Is a Real Drag." *San Francisco Examiner,* 2 November 1979.

Brown, Peter. *Augustine of Hippo.* Berkeley: University of California Press, 1967.

Camus, Albert. *The Plague.* New York: The Modern Library, 1947.

Coburn, Randy Sue. "On the Trail of Ramblin' Jack Elliott." *Esquire Magazine,* April 1984, pp. 80-85.

Connelly, Christopher. "Dylan Makes Another Stunning Comeback." *Rolling Stone,* 24 November 1983, pp. 65-67.

Cott, Jonathan. "Bob Dylan Back in Peak Form." *Rolling Stone,* 16 August 1984, p. 52.

"Dylan: An Irish Storm." *The Tribune* (San Diego), 9 July 1984, A-2.

"Dylan Tour Off to Shaky Start." *Rolling Stone,* 13 December 1979, p. 15.

Editors of Rolling Stone. *The Rolling Stone Interviews.* New York: St. Martin's Press/Rolling Stone Press, 1981.

Eliade, Mircea. *Cosmos and History.* New York: Harper and Row, 1959.

Gray, Michael. *The Art of Bob Dylan.* New York: St. Martin's Press, 1981.

Gross, Michael. *Bob Dylan: An Illustrated History.* New York: Tempo Books, 1980.

Hilburn, Robert. "Bob Dylan at 42—Rolling Down Highway 61 Again." *Los Angeles Times,* Calendar, 30 October 1983, pp. 3-4.

———. "Dylan: 'I Learned That Jesus Is Real and I Wanted That.' " *Los Angeles Times,* Calendar, 23 November 1980, pp. 1,8.

———. "Dylan: The View From Route '84." *Los Angeles Times,* Calendar, 5 August 1984, p. 54.

———. "Dylan's Evangelicalism Goes On." *Los Angeles Times,* 20 November 1979, pt. V, p. 1.

———. "Dylan's New Furor: Rock 'n' Religion." *Los Angeles Times,* Calendar, 18 November 1979, p. 82.

Johnson, Paul. *Modern Times.* New York: Harper and Row, 1983.

Keller, Martin. "Dylan Speaks." *Us* magazine, 2 January 1984, pp. 58-59.

Laurence, Robert. "Dylan Commitment." *The San Diego Union,* 28 November 1979, pt. I, p. A-23.

Lewis, C. S. *Screwtape Letters.* New York: Macmillan, 1961.

Loder, Kurt. "The Rolling Stone Interview: Bob Dylan." *Rolling Stone,* 21 June 1984, pp. 17ff.

McGregor, Craig, ed. *Bob Dylan: A Retrospective.* New York: William Morrow and Co., 1972.

Muggeridge, Malcolm. *The End of Christendom.* Grand Rapids: Eerdmans, 1980.

———. *Jesus, The Man Who Lives.* New York: Harper and Row, 1975.

———. *The Third Testament.* Boston: Little, Brown, 1976.

Nelson, Paul. "Shot of Love, Bob Dylan." *Rolling Stone,* 15 October 1981, p. 61.

Pascal, Blaise. *Pensées.* New York: The Modern Library, 1941.

Rader, Dotson. *I Ain't Marchin' Anymore.* New York: Paperback Library, 1969.

"Random Notes." *Rolling Stone,* 26 July 1979, p. 38.

"Random Notes 1979." *Rolling Stone,* 27 December 1979—10 January 1980, p. 93.

Rinzler, Alan. *Bob Dylan: The Illustrated Record.* New York: Harmony Books, 1978.

Scaduto, Anthony. *Bob Dylan.* New York: New American Library, 1973.

Selvin, Joel. "Bob Dylan's God-Awful Gospel." *San Francisco Chronicle,* 3 November 1979, pt. I, p. 36.

Shepard, Sam. *Rolling Thunder Logbook.* New York: Penguin Books, 1977.

Solzhenitsyn, Aleksandr. *East and West.* New York: Harper and Row, 1980.

"T-Bone Burnett's Rock 'n' Roll Testament." *L.A. Weekly,* 26 March-1 April 1982, p. 16.

Taylor, John. *God Loves Like That!* Richmond, Va.: John Knox Press, 1962.

"The (New) World According to Dylan." *Newsweek,* 17 December 1979, p. 90.

"The Times May Be A-Changin' But Mr. Tambourine Man Shows He'll Always Have Paris." *People,* 16 July 1984, p. 38.

Tucker, Ken. "Dylan's Slow Train of Thought." *Los Angeles Herald Examiner,* Style, 20 November 1979, p.1.

Wenner, Jann. "Best Albums of '79." *Rolling Stone,* 27 December 1979—10 January 1980, p. 124.

———. "Bob Dylan and Our Times: The Slow Train Is Coming." *Rolling Stone,* 20 September 1979, p. 95.

Williams, Paul. *Dylan: What Happened?* Glen Ellen, Calif.: Entwhistle Books, 1980.

"Sad-Eyed Lady of the Lowlands," Copyright © 1966 by Dwarf Music.

"Sara," Copyright © 1975 by Ram's Horn Music.

"Saved," Copyright © 1980 by Special Rider Music.

"Saving Grace," Copyright © 1980 by Special Rider Music.

"Shelter From the Storm," Copyright © 1974 by Ram's Horn Music.

"Shot of Love," Copyright © 1981 by Special Rider Music.

"Slow Train," Copyright © 1979 by Special Rider Music.

"Solid Rock," Copyright © 1980 by Special Rider Music.

"Stuck Inside of Mobile With the Memphis Blues Again," Copyright © 1966 by Dwarf Music.

"Subterranean Homesick Blues," Copyright © 1965 by Warner Bros. Inc.

"Sweetheart Like You," Copyright © 1983 by Special Rider Music.

"Tangled Up in Blue," Copyright © 1974 by Ram's Horn Music.

"Three Angels," Copyright © 1970 by Big Sky Music.

"Trouble in Mind," Copyright © 1979 by Special Rider Music.

"Union Sundown," Copyright © 1983 by Special Rider Music.

"Visions of Johanna," Copyright © 1966 by Dwarf Music.

"Watered Down Love," Copyright © 1981 by Special Rider Music.

"Wedding Song," Copyright © 1973 by Ram's Horn Music.

"What Can I Do for You," Copyright © 1980 by Special Rider Music.

"When He Returns," Copyright © 1979 by Special Rider Music.

"When You Gonna Wake Up," Copyright © 1979 by Special Rider Music.

"Wicked Messenger," Copyright © 1968 by Dwarf Music.

From the album cover *Bringing It All Back Home*—Liner Notes, Copyright © 1965 by Special Rider Music.